Comp@Central

An Anthology of CCSU Student Writing from Writing 100, 105, and 110

2019–2020

XanEdu

XanEdu

4750 Venture Drive, Suite 400
Ann Arbor, MI 48108
800-562-2147
www.xanedu.com

Contents

Research Reports and Annotated Bibliography

Dear Composition Students,

This *Comp@Central* essay collection was designed especially for you. It contains outstanding essays from your fellow students at Central, which they wrote in the very same composition classes you're in now. The essays in this collection were nominated by professors and selected by a committee of English Department faculty members, and they reflect strong (though not perfect) writing from students in Writing 100, 105, and 110 during the 2017–2018 and 2018–2019 academic years.

We hope you'll view this anthology as more than just a reader and use it as you develop your own writing skills; your professor may assign certain essays and use them during class time, but you can also refer to this on your own for models and inspiration. Every piece in the collection begins from an original claim or research question, and most incorporate sources and demonstrate the results of thorough research and sustained consideration of an issue. You will see samples that illuminate complex parts of college writing, such as drafting original thesis statements, synthesizing sources, and organizing longer arguments. So, take notes in the margins. Highlight, underline, and circle parts of the essays. This is a resource for you.

The anthology is organized broadly by genre: reflective essays, arguments, analyses, and research reports and annotated bibliographies. We've carefully curated this collection to be helpful to you as you develop particular writing skills. A new volume gets published each year, so you have an opportunity to be published here in the future!

We received many strong nominations this year, and while we couldn't include them all, we'd like to recognize the following students whose writing was nominated:

Mary Beames	Tesla Lowrey
Madeline Christensen-LeCain	Connor O'Neill
Madison Daddona	Jarod Pazareskis
Leon Green	Elizabeth Perry
Emma Henderson	Myles Place
Gage Kasimir	Anthony Syrek
Jeannette King	Nicole Teti
Jonathan Kryzanski	Lauren Theriault

Sincerely,

The CCSU English Department Composition Committee, 2018–2019

Professor James Austin
Professor Burlin Barr
Professor Elizabeth Brewer Olson
Professor Stephen Cohen
Professor Heidi Eilenberger
Professor Amanda Fields
Professor Amanda Greenwell
Professor Melissa Mentzer
Professor Deborah Spillman

Reflective Essays

Final Portfolio: Critical Reflection

Justin Candido, Writing 100

At the start of this Writing 100 class I lacked the ability to create an effective essay, capitalized by great claims back up with substantial evidence and an analysis to explain further. Along with other essential components such as paragraph structure, transitional phrases, how to stay on task with the essay genre, and even unclear language. While participating in the developmental Writing 100 class I feel as though I have gained the skills throughout the course to enroll in a college level English class. The skills that I have learned have helped me become a more talented writer as shown in the corrections from my very first critiqued essay compared to my final draft of my second major paper.

At the start of the English class I was unable to properly formulate claims that were backed up by evidence and analysis. The main disadvantage I was dealt at the beginning of the class was my under developed knowledge on what a claim really was, such as how it should be formatted and what it signified in the essay as a whole. For example in my first major paper the claim I used stated, "In addition to the college acceptances, I received many more awards during my senior year." This claim is incorrect because it does not serve any significance to what I am proving, and does not promote an argumentative topic for the point I was intending on making. That is incorrect because now that I have been through the class I know that a claim should be promoting an argumentative topic to the paragraph as something to expand, with evidence to back up. Doing this makes the arguments more relatable and easier to understand for the reader.

Along with the progression of ability to formulate claims, I also progressed throughout the semester my ability to use related and effective evidence to back up the arguments I make. In the first essay, my professor left a comment after reviewing my essay which stated, "Try to stay on task. You are trying to tell the reader about your definition of success, your own success, and future success, which you cannot work towards when you shift into generalizations of others." What this meant was that the evidence I used subsequently was not effective to the claim I had made for the paragraph, which seemed to be that I was getting off track to what I was trying to explain in that specific paragraph. Most importantly, by the second major paper, after the essay was critiqued, a more positive comment was left. This note said, "You have made excellent points throughout the paper." "Excellent analysis." through my progression in the class, based on the critiques of my professor, it is evident that I gained the capability to make my arguments stronger by staying on task and providing substantial evidence to the reader exactly what it is I am trying to prove and the points that I am trying to bring up.

Evidentially there has been another skill developed since enrolling in the course as well as the knowledge of claims. The second skill I have obtained throughout the course is paragraph structure. In the first major paper, the scholarship essay, my paragraph structure lacked in the part of the essay where I stated my baseball accolades. In turn, this evidence was not necessarily important to my overall argument that I was trying to convince the reader that I can define success. When referring to paragraph structure, that most importantly points out how the evidence is laid out throughout the entire essay, whether it makes sense for the reader, and the sequence of ideas laid out to make the most sense. Compared to my first major paper, it is evident that there has been much improvement in that part of my writing. In the second major paper, the upside is the evidence flows together to make the reader understand what exactly the points being made are and how they relate to the main argument of the essay. Consequently, an example of this is, "In accompany to the students that come to him, Dante implies that the educational system does not even give the students involved in it their effort to better them and create successful writings." This quote signifies how the structure of the paragraph is started by this quote to set the tone for the rest of the paragraph, tying back into the main argument.

Along with the lack of capability of creating effective paragraph structure, before the start of the course I had a lack of knowledge on transitions to make the essay flow smoothly. Nearly the same importance and purpose of the paragraph structure. In the beginning of the course it is shown that my transitions may not have been effective in the first major paper. For instance, in the first major paper, a transition technique I used was, "In my sophomore year I was inducted into the "National Honor Society." This quote lacks the transitional aspect, which makes the reader struggle to understand how the idea before it, ties into it. As the classed progressed I have shown that the knowledge of transitions and their purposes are being introduced into my work and have become a strong point in my writing. Such as, in my second major paper, the effective transitions I used were, "We can infer that the school systems are failing the students who are already lacking the knowledge of the English language because in Dante's text he voices his opinion when saying." This quote proves that the transitions are effective because the beginning of the quote leads smoothly into what specifically the author stated himself. In turn, this developed technique is vital to the essay to portray a clear image to the reader, which will allow the reader to fully understand how the key points tie together to demonstrate an effective essay.

In conjunction to the progress I made throughout the course, there are also aspects of the writing process that may still need to be improved upon. One of them being limiting the use of unnecessary extra words to explain or introduce an idea in an essay. In the second major paper, an example of this is towards the end of the essay my professor left a specific comment which stated, "you are getting pretty wordy here, which makes the reader do more work to find your meaning. Try to be as direct as possible." This is an aspect of my writing that I feel as though still needs to be improved based on the critiques given because making the reader do more work will distract the reader from the overall goal of understanding the essay as a whole, rather than picking apart each part to try to figure out what it is exactly that is meant for the reader to understand in that specific paragraph.

In the event of more instances to apply the skills that I have learned throughout the course, the process will be much easier, due to the fact that I now have the tools to complete an effective essay. Most recently I have completed multiple essays for other courses. With the knowledge that I have developed, I have applied these keys to the writing process, which in turn made the writing process much easier for me as the writer and easier for the reader to understand. A specific instance where I recently used these tools was in my Criminal Justice research paper. The main topic of that essay the regulation of guns and mental health in society. In this specific essay, the purpose was to explain the methods of policing and theories of policing and criminals tied with the sale of guns, with motive to harm individuals. The aspects of the 100 Writing class came into effect was when we had to explain the methods we thought would apply, and the solutions that we came up with to resolve the gun control conflicts. The main tools that I applied to the essay were claims, paragraph structure, and the initiative to stay on task with what I was trying to prove backed by evidence.

The use of claims played an important role in the essay to explain my stance on the gun control process. As well as other essays, the claims I used were to introduce the main topic that I was intending on emphasizing on in that specific paragraph. For example, "With that way of accessibility, a whole new topic comes about, which is how do you hide the guns from the mentally ill and regulate the sales." This quote directly relates to the use of claims because in this specific quote, there is an argumentative piece introduced where the reader will engage with the text to truly understand the question being posed, which will keep the reader interested and likely will keep reading. Following the use of claims, the second tool to use in the upcoming assignments is the formatting of an effective paragraph structure. Keeping the same essay in mind, the use of an effective paragraph structure was evident when laying out the sequences of paragraphs. This was important for this essay because not only was there one topic to cover in the essay, but there was two. So the use of a good paragraph structure will keep the information in order which will allow the reader to understand.

As the evidence shows there has been many progressions in my knowledge of composing an essay filled with all of the components needed to make a sound argument, followed by the structure built enough to allow the reader to follow along with that I am arguing throughout the paper. These tools will be useful as my college career progresses, to ensure that I create effective essays through all my classes along with my English courses.

Reflection Cover Letter

Reilly Carini, Writing 110

This past semester has been extremely helpful with improving my writing abilities. Before this class I was accustomed to writing in a typically structured five paragraph essay format. This class has enabled me to further develop my writing abilities and structure my papers in different ways. The ability to work together and have discussions with peers allowed me to develop better writing techniques and begin to read my own writing with a critical eye.

For my first writing assignment I stuck to the five paragraph format. I had written about an article previously discussed in class. The article itself was about why the internet is making society stupid. However, I took an opposing stance and argued as to why the internet is actually enriching society and essentially helping it evolve. Reflecting on this piece, I believe I could have enhanced my writing by straying from the five paragraph writing structure by breaking my three supporting arguments into more elaborative paragraphs, instead of having them all bulked together in three separate body paragraphs. This class helped me realize that there are other ways to structure my essays other than using simple five paragraphs. If I were to have broken my essay into multiple paragraphs, it would have organized my writing even better and left room for more elaboration.

During this essay I focused on incorporating quotations and elaborating on them. I came into this class aware of how to use quotes fairly well and used my previous knowledge to improve my writing. However, the peer reviews and the workshops helped me realize where I could improve my usage of quotes throughout my writing. I realized that the opinions of others could open my writing style to many new possibilities.

Two aspects that the peer reviews and the drafts helped me improve were transitions and topic sentences. I realized that the phrasing of both of these would help improve the flow of my writing. In my first draft of my essay the paragraphs were blocked together. For my final draft, by adding transitions, the paragraphs fit together better and easily lead the reader into the next main idea. By my final draft I truly believe I improved the flow and overall structure of my essays, despite the fact that the paragraphs could have been divided into smaller paragraphs.

These workshops and peer reviews also helped with my research paper. I wrote my research paper on body dissatisfaction and the many aspects that contribute to its affects. I made my thesis: the more someone possesses the personality trait of perfectionism, the less satisfied they are with their own body. This writing assignments helped me improve my research from reliable sources. I used the techniques from the previous writing assignment to improve the flow of my paper and made the transitions clearer. I also made sure to break my body paragraphs up into several paragraphs instead of sticking to the five paragraph structure.

The instructive commentary given from my professor was the most helpful. I was able to analyze her comments and improve my writing. I ended up combining some paragraphs and condensing others in order to stick to my thesis. I constructed my paper in a way where I analyzed three different psychological studies to support the idea that mass media is to blame for people's body dissatisfaction and need to seek perfectionism. In my first draft of my research paper the way I wrote my supporting paragraphs sounded very analytical, as if it was from a psychology journal. After my workshop, I edited my research paper by making it sound less scientific and taking less time to explain the study; instead I focused more so on analyzing and evaluating their findings.

In future writing assignments I will make sure to connect back to my thesis throughout the entirety of my writing. I will also try to form topic sentences and closing sentences in a way where they transition easily into my next topic. Both of these aspects will help with the organization of my paper. By organizing my papers better it will keep readers engaged and focused on the main idea at hand without getting lost. Overall, I have built off of my previous writing techniques and improved them throughout this course.

Arguments and Analyses

Misinformation and the Mass Indoctrination of Society

Michael Hill, Writing 110

With the rapid spread of the internet and online media, humanity has made it increasingly efficient to communicate and share information with one another on a global scale. However, with this globalization comes an issue that even the brightest minds in society experience on a daily basis: determining whether information shared on the web has been distorted beyond accuracy. Through poor judgement and a failure to challenge what we read, society has unwittingly continued to plunge itself towards a stark future of gullibility that leaves even experts fearful for democracy. However, as examples such as the 2016 incident "Pizzagate" have proven, fake news can have a critical impact that extends beyond simple naivety. In fact, as new conflicts unravel as a result of misinformation, many individuals have been left questioning how the mass majority of the public could be so credulous as to believe so much of the fake news they encounter. One such explanation is that a mass indoctrination of society has been widely unrecognized due to the public's stubborn prioritization of partisan news over factual sources and a common perception that social media conflict is relatively irrelevant to more serious issues covered by the press. However, this issue cannot be attributed solely to the public. Besides evident failures in filtering out fake news, large scale media platforms are equally responsible due to tactics of emotional manipulation and bold disclaimers that prevent individuals from thinking rationally. Regardless of whether manipulative media platforms or a susceptible audience are more at fault, there is no denying how the collective efforts of both have allowed for the public to be unknowingly indoctrinated with fake news.

Arguably, one of the most prominent reasons for naïve and uncritical belief in inaccurate information is due to the public's stubborn prioritization of partisan news reporting over more reliable and substantiated sources. Rather than value news reporting based on its impartiality and proximity to the truth, society has now increasingly chosen to tune into media that satisfies its own perception of the world by conforming to personal biases. As a result of this confirmation bias, society has taught itself that uncovering the truth really doesn't matter, as long as the information we expose ourselves to encourages us to put more faith in what we already believe. This idea is discussed in the article, "Why Fake News Holds Such Allure" by Story Hinckley when the author mentions a man by the name of Rodney Sparks who had written a book report on World War II in school, using his civilian grandmother's perception of the war at the time as a factual basis for the paper. The author mentions that Sparks had been surprised to see he had failed the assignment due to a lack of historical accuracy. As an explanation, Hinckley explains the relationship that exists between the truth and our own beliefs by stating ". . . lived perception displaces accuracy. In that way, fake news is the ultimatum of a political news culture that has increasingly focused on confirming readers' own worldview instead of challenging them" (Hickley). As individuals such as Spark's grandmother have proven, having a mindset that personal perceptions are more important than proven accuracy is part of the reason that the public is often blind to its own indoctrination. By immediately putting trust in sources that confirm their own predispositions, individuals fail to acknowledge alternative news outlets that might appropriately challenge what they already believe. Although the sources they put faith in might seem accurate according to their own lived perceptions, the unfortunate reality is that the information tends to be construed to support the prejudices of the associated outlet.

In fact, the public often unknowingly accepts unsubstantiated news as the truth because the arising conflict of social media news often seems too irrelevant to recognize when compared to more critical issues covered in the media. In the case of online media platforms, this lack of distinction can be especially seen as a result of the merging of entertainment value with news reporting. Taking Facebook as an example, this platform often presents a distraction from the real world through online amusement. However, it also occasionally provides its viewers with an outlet of news sources that may represent the personal biases of individuals and organizations. Although humans are often skillful at identifying fake news to a certain extent, the intended amusement value of these media platforms can often distract them from the truth in what they read. Even when much of the information being read eventually turns up as being false, very few individuals acknowledge the severity of this social phenomenon. As a result, society continues to be credulous in believing much of the information it reads, allowing for a surreptitious takeover of public opinion by the manipulative news sources. In fact, this issue has become so severe that the public has begun to interpret this phenomenon with the ideas of Marshall McLuhan, a Canadian professor and philosopher known for his studies on mass communication. In relation to the spread of misinformation, McLuhan had predicted that the next world war will be "a guerilla information war with no division between military and civilian participation" (qtd. in Marche). Arguably, the public should be concerned that this idea is already coming to fruition as a result of the aforementioned media platforms. The guerilla war that McLuhan proclaims already exists due to the fake news that furtively seeps into social media. One such example can be seen with the 2016 incident, dubbed "Pizzagate", in which a man by the name of Edgar Maddison Welch fired an assault rifle within a Washington pizzeria in response to fake claims that it had been harboring a sex trafficking ring (Hinckley). Although the situation was diffused with no physical harm done, the incident served to show how the concealed spread of misinformation can even manipulate gullible audiences into committing violent crimes.

However, what the public also fails to acknowledge is how the large-scale news outlets use emotion as a tactic for manipulating society into believing inaccurate information. This is often done by provoking an audience with strong emotions of hate and fear towards a topic and then lacking a factual basis. This idea can be seen in the documentary, "The Brainwashing of My Dad" by Jen Senko when it explains the idea of fearmongering, in which clever word choice and riled up news reporters are used to prevent people from thinking rationally in relation to an issue. According to the documentary, one issue in particular that the emotion tactic has been used on is the idea of ISIS terrorists hiding dormant but ready to strike within the United States. Despite statements like these being debunked by several news stations as a blatant lie, others still claim truth to these news reports. For example, when conflict with ISIS was at its prime, news outlets such as FOX News were responsible for instilling fear in their audience by acting outraged in response to witnessing prayer rugs and korans belonging to the terrorist organization (Senko). However, after debunking the associated photo evidence as nothing more than a red and white Adidas jersey, many viewers remained unconvinced that they were safe from the threat of ISIS. Arguably, this goes to show how provoked emotions can irreversibly prevent individuals from realizing the flaws in their own beliefs. Once these individuals have been terrified by the enraged reactions of news anchors, their lack of rationality that comes next is often enough to permanently shape their perception.

Similarly, a lack of public awareness into how unsubstantiated news has been indoctrinated into society can be attributed with the bold slogans and disclaimers that news sites include to manipulate individuals into accepting their worldviews as the truth. For example, many news stations and media outlets tend to use language within their slogans that, when repeated enough, lead to a less critical or skeptical audience. An example of this can be seen through the usage of phrases such as FOX News's old slogan, "FAIR AND BALANCED," which would be presented across the screen in bold betters and with a patriotic background. By doing so and with enough repetition, it allowed for susceptible viewers to put more faith in the information they report, regardless of the factual accuracy of any given source. However, this issue is especially serious in fake news outlets—such as World News Daily Report—that intentionally prey on credulous viewers through these tactics. For WNDR in particular, this spread of misinformation seems to be especially attributed to the fact that it can use intentionally ironic slogans and headlines to avoid scrutiny for what they call, "the satirical nature of their articles and for the fictional nature of their content" (qtd. in Hinckley). This is often done by presenting the information with disclaimers that proclaim its satirical nature, yet wholly expecting gullible audiences to believe in their absurdly-false reports. Due to the fact that the disclaimers prevent fact-based criticisms from forming, gullible individuals who are unaware of the site's satirical nature might be more likely to read and share these distorted versions of the truth.

In fact, social media users tend to find themselves being vulnerable to the spread of misinformation as a result of large media platforms that fail to filter out fictious content. However, this does not mean that large tech companies have some diabolical plan to manipulate society by means of internet propaganda. In many cases, this issue is simply the result of unintelligent algorithms used in detecting malicious content. One such example can be seen from the TIME Magazine article, entitled "How Your Brain Tricks You into Believing Fake News" by Katy Steinmetz. In this article, Steinmetz discusses how for media giants such as Facebook, faulty media filtration has led to serious financial issues that stem from a decline of public trust. In regard to the spread of fake news, she states "there is no quick fix, though tech companies are under increasing pressure to come up with solutions. Facebook lost more than $120 billion in stock value in a single day in July as the company dealt with a range of issues limiting its growth, including criticism about how conspiracy theories spread on the platform" (Steinmetz). Considering the fact that many gullible social media users tend to pay little attention beyond headlines and minute details of the articles they share, it is no surprise how faulty algorithms are partly responsible for the public's indoctrination of fake news. Since the public tends to blindly trust the information it is shown on media platforms like Facebook and Twitter, its is not always obvious when failures in news filtration have allowed less substantiated sources to seep into the media feed. As a result, the fake news is able to spread between gullible parties with a high expectation for its accuracy.

However, opponents may claim that the public does in fact notice when misinformation is present but chose not to care due to its evident appeal to their own personal mindsets. According to this argument, individuals tend to be fully aware of what is factually correct but feel that accuracy is irrelevant when compared to the unsubstantiated ideologies that make them feel good about themselves (Sparks). While it is true to say that individuals tend to be biased towards information that reaffirms what they already believe, this does not mean that they are consciously aware of their own confirmation bias. Instead, confirmation bias can work more like a covert prison, constricting ingenuous individuals from working past their prejudices or thinking rationally. A great example of this idea can be seen with satirical news organizations that—despite obvious disclaimers against their content—continue to successfully convince audiences of their accuracy. Arguably, this is due to the fact that their own lived perception clouds their ability to think clearly when the truth is right there in front of them. No matter how many disclaimers are presented, having an ideological bias makes even the most ludicrous claims and prejudices seem logical.

In regard to inaccurate information, a mass indoctrination of the public has been widely unrecognized due to the collective efforts of manipulative news outlets and a susceptible audience. Most commonly, this issue has resulted from the public's desire for information that reaffirms its own preexisting beliefs. In fact, through everyday interaction with social media, the public has also contributed to this conflict with its neglect for the severity of fake news. However, this global phenomenon cannot be solely pinpointed to the gullibility of the public. Through the means of satirical disclaimers, emotional manipulation and faulty news filtration, large media corporations concurrently contribute to this epidemic. In response, society must now collectively decide on its own tactics to employ in the fight for objective truth-seeking. One such approach is to start teaching society to shame news corporations and individuals that spread dangerously disruptive lies within the country. Promoting these lies isn't just creating a naïve society; it's terrifying audiences into acting out against irrational threats—such as dormant ISIS terrorists and non-existent government conspiracies. Although finding a virtually infallible approach to this issue is no easy task, coming together now as a well-informed community may be what it takes to prevent humanity's eventual demise.

Works Cited

Hinckley, Story. "Why Fake News Holds Such Allure." The *Christian Science Monitor*, 15 Dec. 2016, www.csmonitor.com/USA/Politics/2016/1215/Why-fake-news-holds-such-allure.

Marche, Stephen. "Why Is the U.S. So Susceptible to Social-Media Distortion?" The *New Yorker*, 31 Oct. 2017, www.newyorker.com/culture/cultural-comment/why-is-the-us-so-susceptible-to-social-media-distortion.

Senko, Jen, director. *The Brainwashing of My Dad*. Produced by Matthew Modine, Dedos Peliculas, 2016.

Steinmetz, Katy. "How Your Brain Tricks You into Believing Fake News." *TIME Magazine*, 9 Aug. 2018, time.com/5362183/the-real-fake-news-crisis/.

"Say It Ain't So": An Argument against Allowing PED Users in the Baseball Hall of Fame

Keegan Jarvis, Writing 110

A performance-enhancing drug is defined as "a substance that is used illicitly to improve athletic performance" (Merriam-Webster). Performance-enhancing drugs are taken by athletes in order to gain a competitive advantage over those they compete against. These drugs have become notorious for their role in baseball. Many record setting baseball players, such as Barry Bonds and Roger Clemens, have tested positive for PEDs multiple times throughout their careers, and have become scorned in baseball circles. These players from the "Steroid Era" are now eligible to be elected into the Baseball Hall of Fame and there is much debate on whether or not known PED users should be recognized as important participants of the game. Because many users were record setting players, some fans and sports analysts argue that their records should be reflected in the Hall of Fame. However, given the unnatural competitive advantage PED users possessed, the damage they will do to the integrity of the Hall of Fame, and the potential danger they may cause to future athletes who may emulate their criminal activity, proven PED users must be banned from the Hall of Fame.

Opponents of banning PED users from the Baseball Hall of Fame make several arguments. First, opponents argue that PEDs use is a part of baseball history, and since the Baseball Hall of Fame tells the story of the game, leaving out PED users would be choosing to ignore a significant part of baseball's past. The period of baseball history from the early 90's to early 2000's is commonly referred to as the "Steroid Era" due to the high number of alleged users and the banning of steroids in 2003. Leaving these players out, they argue, would be choosing not to acknowledge this timeframe. Next, they contend that players who previously used PEDs are already enshrined in the Hall of Fame, so removing them or banning future players would be unfair. For example, Hall of Fame third baseman Mike Schmidt admitted to using amphetamines, or greenies, "a couple of times" during his career (Chass 1). Schmidt has remained in the Hall of Fame ever since being inducted in 1995. Finally, they insist that PED users set records, regardless of PED use, and these records should be reflected in the Hall of Fame. For example, Barry Bonds currently holds the record for most home runs in a career, with 762, but is not in the Hall of Fame because he has been accused of using performance enhancing drugs. Opponents argue that because he holds this prestigious record, he should be enshrined in the Baseball Hall of Fame, but honoring proven users like Barry Bonds would only glorify the use of performance enhancing drugs while tarnishing the reputation of America's game.

Barry Bonds and other performance enhancing users must be banned from the Baseball Hall of Fame because PEDs grant users an unfair competitive advantage over other players. As stated in the article, "Don't let cheaters into baseball's Hall of Fame" in the *Washington Post*, "PEDs . . . have an advantage that other players do not enjoy" (*Don't let cheaters into baseball's Hall of Fame* 1). This means that PEDs grant users a competitive advantage that not all other players have. This is important because it proves that use of PEDs is essentially an immoral cheat code, granting users the ability to hit more home runs or strike out more batters. Since users have an unfair advantage, they are able to easily get the better of players who do not use PEDs. PED users therefore can become difference makers in close games. This statement is echoed by Don Yaeger of Forbes, who states, "It's not the fact that they [PED users] cheated. It's the fact that opponents lost due to their cheating" (1). In other words, Yaeger is saying that PED users were able to exploit those who did not use PEDs, and were able to help their team win games. This is critical because when someone like Barry Bonds, who currently holds the MLB record for most home runs in a career and has been linked to PEDs throughout said career, is up for election into the Hall of Fame, voters must consider how his actions potentially changed the course of history. Furthermore, Richard McLaren, of *Marquette Sports Law Review*, states, "Winning athletes who do not dope want their results to be worthy of admiration, not skeptics and innuendo" (8). Here, the author is saying that athletes who do not use performance enhancing drugs want their records to hold value, not be accused of cheating in order to obtain these records. This is essential to the argument because it proves that even players themselves acknowledge that PED users have an advantage over non-users. These same players also want their own records to hold more value than the records of those that use PEDs. As these points demonstrate, PED users gain an unfair competitive advantage over players who don't use PEDs.

Another reason users should be banned from the Baseball Hall of Fame is because PEDs ruin the integrity of the game, and will therefore tarnish the integrity of the Hall of Fame. As stated in the article, *Don't let cheaters into baseball's Hall of Fame* in the Washington Post, "Baseball's Hall of Fame in Cooperstown, NY is the sport's pantheon to its greatest players, but not only that; it is kind of a national shrine" (*Don't let cheaters into baseball's Hall of Fame* 1). This means that the Baseball Hall of Fame is a very important part of the game of baseball, to the point where even casual fans will make the trip to Cooperstown to see it. This is essential information because it establishes the integrity of the Baseball Hall of Fame, and further establishes how PED users being inducted into the Hall of Fame would compromise its image. The article further states that, "Rules should not be suspended for a [PED using] batter who hit enough home runs, or a [PED using] pitcher whose fastball was unhittable. To do that would make a mockery of the rules, and of baseball, and of Cooperstown (*Don't let cheaters into baseball's Hall of Fame* 1). In other words, any notion of allowing PED users into the Baseball Hall of Fame simply because they were great players is unacceptable. They used PEDs, which is against the rules of baseball. This is critical because it further proves that the Baseball Hall of Fame has a high level of integrity, and allowing PED users to be enshrined in it would cause significant damage to that integrity. Furthermore, Richard H. McLaren, a writer for *Marquette Sports Law Review*, states, "the integrity of sport is vulnerable to the intrusion by a minority of individuals who promote or engage in the use of performance enhancing drugs" (2). Here, McLaren argues that the integrity of sports can be hurt by those who engage in PED use. This is essential to the argument because if players can ruin the integrity of a sport by using PEDs, they can just as easily ruin the integrity of the Baseball Hall of Fame by being inducted. As these points indicate, PED usage undermines the honor of the game of baseball, and if those who engage in the practice are inducted, will therefore damage the reputation of the Baseball Hall of Fame.

Perhaps the most convincing reason PED users should be banned from the Baseball Hall of Fame is due to the damaging precedent it may set for the future players of the game. As Don Yaeger states, "What type of example would we be setting if we allowed these tarnished legends into the most sacred inner circle that the sport of baseball possesses?" (1). The author is saying that allowing players who have used PEDs throughout their careers, such as Barry Bonds or Roger Clemens, would set a bad example for future athletes. This is important because despite youth today not growing up watching these now scorned players, seeing their enshrining in the Baseball Hall of Fame may indirectly encourage them to turn to performance enhancing drugs. Bill Shaikin of the LA times supports a ban of PED users, stating "No longer would kids see juiced up sluggers as role models" (1). The author is saying that banning PED users from the Hall of Fame would cast a negative shadow over them, and youth would no longer see them as players to look up to. This is critical because if the platform these scorned players have is taken away, they cannot negatively influence younger athletes. The dangerous influence of glorified drug users on the minds of young athletes is explored by Daniel Healey of the *Marquette Sports Law Review* who describes the impact that Mark McGwire had on young players. During an interview, a *New York Times* reporter saw a bottle of androstenedione, a common over-the-counter supplement, in McGwire's locker. Androstenedione, or andro, has a chemical similarity to many illegal anabolic steroids. After the interview was published, "given McGwire's enormous popularity, it was not surprising that the discovery increased andro sales by 500%" (297). In other words, because Mark McGwire, one of the most popular players in the MLB, took an over-the-counter supplement with similarities to anabolic steroids, young athletes believed that they should take the same drug in order to be as good as their favorite player. This is critical because it proves that professional athletes have a huge impact on younger athletes, and can influence them to do something that could potentially destroy their body.

As these points confirm, PED users should be banned from the Hall of Fame in order to discourage young athletes from taking illegal drugs.

As these arguments make clear, PED users should be banned from the Baseball Hall of Fame. While the opposition argues that PED use is a part of baseball's history, several arguments undermine the legitimacy of their assertions. First, PED users should be banned from the Baseball Hall of Fame because PED use destroys the integrity of the game of baseball, and therefore the Hall of Fame. This argument is valid because PEDs are banned substances, so allowing those who use PEDs into the Baseball Hall of Fame would undermine the value of being inducted. Second, PED users should be banned from the Baseball Hall of Fame because PEDs grant users a competitive advantage over players who do not use PEDs. This argument is valid because players like Barry Bonds and Alex Rodriguez, both alleged PED users, hold MLB records, meaning that steroids easily could've helped them. Finally, PED users should be banned from the Baseball Hall of Fame because banning convicted PED users would discourage future athletes from using PEDs. This argument is valid because there are examples of players getting caught using over-the-counter substances resembling PEDs, and sales of these substances increased greatly. The game of baseball is America's game, and in many ways it is a representation of our nation's values. Lines between fair and foul are clearly drawn on the baseball diamond, and this same clarity must apply to the induction of honorees in the Hall of Fame. To allow men who have operated outside the fair rules of the game to be honored is a violation that will affect the game and its players for years to come. To conclude, PED users must be banned from the Baseball Hall of Fame, because only the best, most moral players should have the privilege of being enshrined in baseball history.

Works Cited

Chass, Murray. "Schmidt an Open Book on Greenies," *The New York Times*, 28 February 2006

Healey, Daniel. "Fall of the Rocket: Steroids in Baseball and the Case Against Roger Clemens," *Marquette Sports Law Review*, vol. 19, 2008

McLaren, Richard H. "Is Sport Losing Its Integrity?," *Marquette Sports Law Review*, vol. 21, no. 2, Spring 2011

"Performance-enhancing drug," Merriam-Webster.com. Merriam-Webster, 2011.

Shaikin, Bill. "Baseball Hall of Fame might no longer be off limits for MLB steroid-era players," *LA Times*, 13 January 2017

Washington Post Editorial Board. "Don't let cheaters into baseball's Hall of Fame," *Washington Post*, 6 January 2017

Yaeger, Don. "How the Baseball Hall of Fame is Protecting Its Integrity From Cheaters," *Forbes*, 30 January 2018

Is "Organic" Really Organic?

Amy Glover, Writing 110

The interest in organic foods has risen in the past decade. With more and more people resorting to healthier choices, it is necessary that consumers be cautious about where they spend their dollar. While the pros and cons list seems to be heavy on the pro side, there are many secrets that lie behind the word "organic." It is because of these mysteries that something must be done. Organic food must be more heavily regulated to create accurate labeling, reinforce farms that practice good standards, and increase consumer safety.

Growth of the organic movement has consumers striving to eat well and live a healthy lifestyle. It appears that news reports more often talk about the problems of conventional food each week and discover a new one that supposedly causes cancer. Foods that are labeled "organic" alongside the United States Department of Agriculture's seal of approval are, by law, food without pesticides, herbicides, synthetic fertilizers, hormones, radiation, and antibiotics (Chenglin 364). Organic food has an interesting history in that it existed before it actually existed. Before the 1920s, all farming was technically organic. No one had the means of operation that we do today. Everything was done by hand and by a person. During the industrialization of agriculture after World War II, chemicals and pesticides were discovered to lessen the burden of insects and weeds around crops. With that, and the use of mechanized machinery, farming was never the same. It was not until roughly the

1970s that "organic farming" in the United States became a trend once again (Chenglin 352). Consumers realized that what farmers were doing and what was going into the food could not be healthy, despite the benefits for a farmers' business. More farms began to produce organically once again, even though the challenge to compete with big business farms was daunting.

The need for accurate organic labels is evident. Due to lenient regulations, farmers are able to find loopholes to cheat the system and claim their foods are "organic" when they actually are not. This deceit is a huge problem because consumers are paying more money for something they *believe* to be healthier. For example, research conducted by Reid Harvey, Christine Zakhour and Hannah Gould, discovered that "certain exemptions allow products to be labeled organic without [USDA] certification" (1956). This generally occurs with smaller farms that are local to the store they are selling in. If the USDA refined their regulations and added more specific rules this would not be an issue. Many consumers not only try to buy organic, but also local, and with these tricks, many are convinced that what they purchase for their family is healthier. Accurate labels would create less worry for consumers and a higher integrity of the food organic farmers are producing.

Another misconception behind the labeling process is how foods do not have to be entirely organic to be labeled organic. The phrase, "made with organic . . ." might sound familiar, and to most, it might not mean much. However, according to Liu Chenglin from the *Stanford Journal of International Law*, "under the particular regulations, there are three layers of organic products" (341). Of these, there is one, "100% organic"; two, "organic" meaning 95% or more; and three, "made with organic" which can be anything from 70% to 95% organic substance. (Chenglin

341). Despite these tiers having very different meanings, all three may be labeled the same in the store, whether that is the word "organic" or the USDA's seal. Unfortunately, this means the consumer is left without all the information on the product they are buying and therefore being deceived once again. With more attention to how these products are labeled, there would be a decrease in the amount of food available that is organic. As a result, the choices that are left would be authentic and leave consumers without any concern on the quality and healthiness of their food.

Not all farmers are playing fast and loose with the regulations, so it is important to give those farmers a fair system to sell their products in. Organic farming is not easy to do. The extra time and money it takes are factors in the decision for farmers looking to appeal to a growing demographic. Elizabeth Weise, a journalist from *USA Today*, talks about how "organic foods typically have lower yields per acre than conventional agriculture." This decreased output is primarily due to the fact that the methods prohibited in organic farming are those that make conventional farming easier, such as growth hormones and pesticides. Farmers put in more personal effort and time, ensuring that the food you buy at the grocery store is up to standards and tastes just as good. It is not fair to have some farmers abide by the rules and regulations and some not, while all receive the benefits of being consider am "organic farmer." Strictly enforcing the regulations in place could ease these tensions.

Additionally, the cost to maintain an organic farm in both labor and certification is pricey. As previously stated, there are extra output times and manual labor involved in organic farming than there is in conventional farming. Therefore, consumers could then assume it is more expensive to pay employees at organic farms, on average. Unfortunately, that is not the only cost restraint involved. To obtain an organic certification, an agent will inspect the farm, and if it passes, give the farm its seal of approval. These certifications can cost "anywhere from $400.00 to $1000.00 annually for small farms" (Weise). A "small farm" is generally one with 179 acres or less. While this may seem like a small fee, when farms are compared to thousands of other "small farms" around the area, it can be difficult to stand out. One might sympathize with small business owners like these farmers. It can be difficult enough trying to compete with others on such a large scale without worrying about those who may be doing so unfairly. Having a "USDA organic seal" can be a huge leg up and allows farmers to charge more for the products they offer. Implementing improved guidelines of what can be called "organic" and which farmers are producing in good standards is a win-win for farmers and consumers alike.

Along with increased regulation, more safety, could come for consumers. Since there are so many tricks and shortcuts used by farmers and the government agencies regulating them, it is no shock that there are myths about organic food. The fact that consumers do not understand that these are myths can impair their safety. For instance, "consumers are often not aware that organic standards do not directly address food safety considerations such as microbial or chemical hazards" (Harvey et al., 1956). What this is saying, is that even organic food can cause issues such as food borne illness. This is just one of the many misconceptions about organic food. Creating more thorough regulations not only on how the food is produced, but also how it is transported and handled could address issues like this and as a result increase consumer safety.

Some may disagree and say that the regulations and restrictions placed on organic farms are satisfactory and anymore intervention would just be a nuisance. At some level consumers should be self-reliant and if they cared more about where their food came from, they could find out, and buy from somewhere else, if they were not pleased with the results. For example, many people might not know that "40% of organic foods consumed in the United States are imported from over 100 foreign countries" (Chenglin 333). Currently, there are no rules indicating how specific or transparent labeling for organic products must be. It might not be required that such a circumstance be reported alongside a "USDA organic seal," but would doing so really effect consumers' buying decisions? Required or not, consumers would most likely be interested in knowing the truth.

Despite this argument, I maintain that organic food needs to be held to higher standards for the sake of the consumer. There is too much unreliability when it comes to the foods we buy. It is imperative that consumers are given, in full detail, where their food came from to be able to make a smart and sound decision. For example, Whole Foods should not be allowed to label their products as "locally grown organic" when "locally" really means 7,000 miles away in China (Chenglin 335). There is a stark difference between self-reliance and deception.

In conclusion, the benefits of increasing regulation and being upfront about a product largely outweigh the negatives. Consumers want the truth about what they are feeding to their families every day. Farmers should be able to sell their product without worry of deceptive competition and our food should be safer. As stated earlier, organic food has existed long before people started caring about it. But will we ever be able to obtain such a pure form of organic as it was originally? Be careful the next time you take a trip to the grocery store.

Works Cited

Chenglin, Liu. "Is USDA Organic" a Seal of Deceit?: The Pitfalls of USDA Certified Organics Produced in the United States, China and Beyond." *Stanford Journal of International Law,* vol. 47, no. 2, Summer 2011, pp. 333–378. *Academic Search Premiere,* search.ebscohost.com/login.aspx? direct=true&db=aph&AN=66621 661&site=ehost-live&scope=site.

Harvey, R. Reid, et al. "Foodborne Disease Outbreaks Associated with Organic Foods in the United States." *Journal of Food Protections,* vol. 79, no. 11, Nov. 2016, pp. 1953–1958. *Academic Search Premiere,* doi:10.4315/0362-028X.JFP-16-204.

Weise, Elizabeth. "Is Organic Always Best?." *USA Today,* Dec. 2010, n.p. *Academic Search Premiere,*search.ebscohost.com/login.aspx?direct=true&db=aph&AN= J0E358494451510&site=ehost-live&scope=site.

The Successful Version of Gentrification

Jenna Keegan, Writing 110

According to Darei Ross, "'Gentrification is when opportunity moves into a neighborhood and that opportunity is not directly for or in line with the indigenous population of that neighborhood'" (qtd in Dougherty 2). Given both its benefits and disadvantages, the process is controversial. On one hand, gentrification can increase economic development and tax revenue while decreasing crime in the long run. On the other hand, gentrification poses challenges for existing residents to keep up with higher priced housing and stores, or, if adjustments are not possible, being displaced. On balance, considering both its potential for economic gain and the possible harm to current residents, gentrification should be allowed if it's introduced into neighborhoods gradually and with restrictions.

Opponents of this position make several arguments. First, they argue that gentrification to any degree pushes out locals and makes their lives more difficult through dramatic change. Next, they insist that gentrification results in cohabation of people of opposite social and financial status, causing conflict within communities. Finally, they maintain that gentrification needs to be unregulated or there will not be any progress. Dramatic gentrification is required for change. For all these reasons, opponents reach conclusions at opposite ends of the spectrum, that gentrification should be unregulated, or not allowed at all.

One reason gentrification should not be stopped but should be regulated is because it increases economic success and tax revenue by boosting the amount of businesses in the area. According to Ehren Wynder, "Ross claimed gentrification is revitalization without the benefits of revitalization returning to the community" (2). This supports my thesis because revitalization is essentially gentrification with regulations set in place to protect members of the community. This is important because if cities are gentrified using a revitalizing approach, cities will reap the benefits without residents feeling any negative impact. If residents can stay in their homes, get jobs or own businesses, and have access to public services, such as an affordable transportation system, everyone will benefit from gentrification. Additionally, Dougherty explains, "The influx of money is creating new jobs in hotels and restaurants as traditional industries like farming and timber fade out" (2). This means that would be more jobs tailored to not only older people who have worked there their entire lives, but all ages. Older resident who can't handle the hard labor of farming and timber can also appreciate these jobs. This is important because it provides opportunities for older people to work longer, younger people to find jobs they can do, and even injured or handicap people to have jobs available to them. This will not only benefit those specific people, but the economy overall, because businesses would have enough employees to grow and succeed financially. O'Neill added, "Gentrification is a double-edged sword. It's hard on renters when the cost of housing does up, but it can be a godsend to poor homeowners ready and willing to sell" (2). The author is saying that many renters have issues with high expenses after gentrification, but the issue can be controlled with regulations. It is also a very good situation to be in as home owner, because many companies are looking to buy property. This is significant because with only a few changes to how gentrification is introduced into cities, it could help every resident, renter or homeowner. Together, these points demonstrate how controlled gentrification can create more tax revenue and economic success for the city.

Another reason gentrification should be allowed but regulated is because it helps decrease crime long-term in cities. As Sylla states, "Gentrification hardly would have had anything to do with [an increase in substandard apartments]. Instead, suburban sprawl and neighborhood neglect largely are responsible for that, with the willing cooperation of disinvestment, crime, drugs, vagrancy and higher property taxes." This supports my thesis because crime is increased by neighborhood neglect. Less pride in a neighborhood, empty houses, and a lack of authority enforcing laws create opportunities for criminals to act with no consequence. Neighborhood neglect happens when gentrification doesn't happen at all and the city has little money, as well as when gentrification is left unregulated, because companies buy property and neglect it. This is important because the best option to avoid neighborhood neglect is by allowing gentrification but enforcing rules that prevent abandoned property. Lee added, "Sampson, Raudenbush, and Earls argue that 'residential tenure and homeownership promote collective efforts to maintain social control', thereby engendered collective efficacy, where social cohesion among neighbors, combined with a willingness to intervene for the common good, results in decreased violence" (1). This means that gentrification leads to more prideful neighborhoods, which causes residents to want to keep their area crime free. This is important because when people want to stop crime, people will be far more inclined to avoid the area for criminal activities. Over time, the criminal rate would continue to decrease. The author further explains, "In the long term, therefore, it is expected that homeownership-related gentrification, where households with vested interests and relatively greater resources to effectively organize for services, should eventually bring about decreased crime in the lower income areas where gentrifiers decide to locate" (1). In other words, areas that have resources provided to them eventually have a decrease in rates of crime. This is relevant because neighborhoods that are gentrified generate business and money, so they have services provided and resources available. This is what residents need for them to accept gentrification at all. As these points make clear, gentrification can benefit cities by providing more neighborhood moral and ultimately lowering crime rates.

One exception to this argument is that gentrification can cause displacement of residents; therefore, there should be regulations on when and how gentrification happens in cities. According to David Allen, "neighborhood groups said they wanted a new nonprofit housing organization because the existing ones seemed only concerned with building new houses and not engaging in the community or providing opportunities" (qtd in Wynder 2). This supports my thesis because it demonstrates how residents are not usually angry about the occurrence of gentrification, but they want it to be done in a way that benefits the community. This is important because if there were regulations that supported locals, existing residents would welcome the process, a shift which would reduce the controversy surrounding gentrification and of benefit to everyone. The author further states, "Haynes added that there's also an 'unspoken problem' with houses laying vacant because the investment groups that own them find it cheaper to sit on them rather than maintain them on the market. Allen confirmed Haynes' point, saying [Grand Rapids, Michigan] has identified about 800 single-family homes that are vacant" (3). This means that large companies buy the houses of local people who can't afford to stay when their neighborhood is gentrified. Simultaneously, they are keeping houses off the market, while allowing them to deteriorate until they are no longer livable. They do this because it is cheaper than maintaining the houses and property, even when renting or selling them. This is critical because if regulations were passed that prevented investors from buying that much property without using it, there would be fewer houses sitting empty and families looking for homes unsuccessfully. It would also decrease the chance of empty houses being used for crime, such as vandalism or drugs. Wynder adds, "Ross said he was more concerned with identifying opportunities in a given community and formulating policies specifically designed for each community" (3). This means that appropriate regulations are essential to successful gentrification and that these regulations need to be tailored to the needs of particular communities. This is important because if regulations were set based on the requirements of a community, it would be more successful and residents would benefit, rather than struggle or be displaced. As these points demonstrate, community residents will welcome gentrification and are more apt to benefit from it if protective regulations are passed.

As these arguments indicate, with controlled restrictions specified to each city, gentrification should be allowed. While the opposition argues that any gentrification causes displacement, gentrification introduces people of different status causing conflict, and only dramatic change can cause any progress in cities several arguments invalidate the legitimacy of their assertions. First, gentrification is not only detrimental because it often leads to more supply and demand in new businesses, leading to higher economic success and tax revenue for the city. Second, gentrification is sometimes beneficial because it can lead to a decrease in crime in cities. Finally, gentrification needs to be controlled with regulations because residents need to be able to adjust to the change financially and socially. To conclude, gentrification may provide many cities and the residents benefits in the future if introduced correctly.

Works Cited

Dougherty, Conor. "The New American Gentry; Wealthy Folks are Colonizing Rural Areas, Bringing Cash, Culture—and Controversy." *Wall Street Journal*, Jan 19, 2008. ProQuest, https://ccsu.idm.oclc.org/login?url=https://search-proquest-com.ccsu.idm.oclc.org/docview/399021146?accountid=9970.

O'Neill, Brian. "Is Gentrification Better than No Gentrification?" *Pittsburgh Post-Gazette*, Oct 25, 2018. ProQuest, https://ccsu.idm.oclc.org/login?url=https://search-proquest-com.ccsu.idm.oclc.org/docview/2124686654?accountid=9970.

RUSSELL, JAMES. "There Goes the Neighborhood: Can Gentrification Improve Urban Communities without Pushing out Longtime Residents?" *Architectural Record*, vol. 206, no. 10, Oct. 2018, pp. 96–98. EBSCOhost, search.ebscohost.com/login.aspx?direct=true&db=aph&AN=132093270&site=ehost-live&scope=site.

Steinmetz-Wood, Madeleine, et al. "Is Gentrification All Bad? Positive Association between Gentrification and Individual's Perceived Neighborhood Collective Efficacy in Montreal, Canada." *International Journal of Health Geographics*, vol. 16, July 2017, pp. 1–8. EBSCOhost, doi:10.1186/s12942-017-0096-6.

Sylla, Cheikh T. "Changing Neighborhoods Need Changing Perspectives Series: GUEST COLUMN." *St.Petersburg Times*, Nov 10, 1990, pp. 22. *ProQuest*, https://ccsu.idm.oclc.org/login?url=https://search-proquest-com.ccsu.idm.oclc.org/docview/262785169?accountid=9970.

Wynder, Ehren. "Public Panel Scrutinizes Gentrification." *Grand Rapids Business Journal*, vol. 35, no. 47, 2017, pp. 1-1,6. *ProQuest*, https://ccsu.idm.oclc.org/login?url=https://search-proquest-com.ccsu.idm.oclc.org/docview/1970110375?accountid=9970.

The Millennial Stereotype

Joseph Pille, Writing 110

Stereotypes are alive and well in the 21st century, and few have been more prevailing than that of the young millennial American. Despite the meaningful contributions made to society by young people in recent times, the images of a college student at a Bernie Sanders rally demanding free tuition, or a young man taking a selfie with a hijacker on board an airliner have been repeatedly engrained into American minds by the media so as to classify exactly what a millennial is. The news media would like Americans to believe that millennials are all entitled and lacking moral values, yet it is impossible to categorize an entire generation under just one single stereotype, and millennials are no exception.

What exactly is a millennial? If using the term to define a member of a particular age group, it would be someone born in the 80's or 90's who grew up during the early part of the new millennium. The term however, has many negative connotations that describe much more than just a person's age. To name a few; millennials are often stereotyped as being lazy, entitled, liberal thinking, or a combination of them all (Green). In addition, they have been branded as the social media generation, a cell phone addicted bunch with priorities like having the most followers on Instagram trumping values such as hard work and dedication that are more important in the real world. Despite the accomplishments made by people in the millennial generation, such as the Medal of Honor Kyle

Carpenter earned for throwing himself on a grenade to save his brother's life in Afghanistan, the media seems to reserve the term for the more negative aspects of the group than positive. That young marine will never be referred to as a millennial in the news, but the term will certainly be tossed around when drawing a comparison between Kim Kardashian and the young women who aspire to have a social media presence as big as hers (Glass-Katz). This is important because it makes an association with the values of the generation with a public figure who is known for having almost none, and has helped to cast a stereotype on young twenty-something's that will likely stick for some time.

Inducing fear in their audience is one of the primary ways the media keeps stereotypes alive. A rational viewer knows better than to assume that all members of another group fit a certain categorization perfectly, but a fearful viewer may worry about how that other groups actions might affect themselves. When this happens, logic and reason often takes a backseat. Imagine a well off, middle aged man who worked hard to be successful and enjoy the fruits of his labor. To him, knowing that a group of young liberal voters were pushing to increase the amount of taxes he must pay on his income would not be seen as good. Rather than attempting to understand how many young people share that ideology, it is much easier for a news network to instill fear in this man to put distance between him and the group being stereotyped. This would make him want to vote accordingly to counteract. Fox News has nearly written the playbook for this method in their documentation of rallies in support of Bernie Sanders, where one of the largest themes of the campaign is free college tuition for young people at the expense of the American taxpayer. Rather than going to schools and interviewing students to get their opinions, clips of students protesting for free tuition are ran over and over again. Because of this, many Americans now believe that all college students must be voting for Bernie Sanders, and want to raise taxes on the rich as well.

Projecting the faults and misdoings of a group is another method used to perpetuate the stereotype against millennials. By repeatedly highlighting the mistakes made by people in a certain category, the networks can attack that group and continue to reinforce that stereotype without even using the groups name. A perfect example of this was when EgyptAir Flight 181 was hijacked in late March 2016, by a man wearing what he claimed to be was a suicide vest. Rather than attempting to subdue the hijacker, a 26-year-old male passenger decided to take a selfie with him instead (Fox News). The picture was plastered all over Facebook by nearly every news outlet in existence as an example of what millennial values are, that social media fame was potentially more important than saving the lives of his fellow passengers and himself. This was a stark contrast to the passengers on board United Airlines Flight 93, who overthrew their own hijackers on 9/11 and crashed the plane into the ground instead of a building full of people. Given the 15-year gap between the two events, it was the perfect opportunity for media outlets to highlight the increasing divide in morals from one generation to the next.

None of these tactics would work however if the theme of what a millennial is wasn't repeated. If the media only covered one aspect of the millennial generation periodically, the stereotype would not stick. Instead, articles and news clips with a reoccurring theme are repeated to reinforce the stereotype. Take the job finding website Monster.com for example, which is heavily used by employers and job seekers as well. In Monster's article "Millennials, These Are The 5 Stereotypes You're Up

Against At Work", it puts out in broad daylight the negative stereotypes associated with the millennial generation (Bortz). Common sense would have an employer basing their opinions of a potential employee on the interview. But by pushing the issue, Monster is telling employers exactly what to expect from a millennial before they even meet them.

Stereotypes exist partially because of the efforts made by others to keep them alive, and by those who choose to buy into them. While there are instances where millennials fit into the stereotype as perfectly as the hijacker selfie, there have been too many accomplishments made by this generation to put all of us into a single categorization. Despite logical Americans believing that the actions and beliefs of a select few members of a group do not represent them all, the media has done their part to counter rational thinking to push the stereotype for their own agenda. Until more positive associations with this generation are made, such as the Marine in Afghanistan, or even an employee proving their boss' expectations wrong, then the millennial stereotype will likely follow us for the rest of our lives.

Works Cited

Bortz, Daniel. "Millennials, These Are the 5 Stereotypes You're up against at Work" *Monster.com*. Monster.com, 17 Nov. 2015. Web. 04 Apr. 2016. (Highlighted how employers view millennials and how the stereotype continues to be perpetuated in the professional world).

Fox News. "'Selfie of a Lifetime': Man Gets a Photo With Egyptian Airline Hijacker." *Fox News Insider*. Fox News, 30 Mar. 2016. Web. 04 Apr. 2016. (Used as an example to show how the media continues to reinforce the stereotype and make an example of one person).

Glass-Katz, Ally. "Let Them Eat Kake: Kim Kardashian a Millennial Monarch—
The Bowdoin Orient." *The Bowdoin Orient*. The Bowdoin Orient, 28 Feb. 2014.
Web. 04 Apr. 2016. (Reinforced my claim that the media believes millennials
lack values by comparing them with reality TV star Kim Kardashian).

Green, Alison. "5 Workplace Stereotypes About Millennials That Aren't True." *US
News RSS*. US News, 16 Mar. 2015. Web. 04 Apr. 2016. (The article reinforced
my assertion that all Millennials cannot be categorized into one stereotype).

Stranger Danger? Probably Not: The Way We Treat Sexual Child Abuse within the Home and Raising Awareness

Gabriella Reyes, Writing 105

Casa de Menor is a Brazil-based organization that is concerned with neglected and abused children that created a PSA trying to get the point across that sexual child abuse is an experience that causes permanent trauma. The image is of a clean and tidy living room. It is a basic living room with tables, chairs, and photos in it. Everything is in place except for a lone teddy bear slightly beneath the couch. In the center of the room is a young girl looking directly in the camera. Her face has no expression but forces the viewer to look at her. She holds a disheveled doll in her hand. There are adult hands draped on her from her chest to her knees and they continue down onto the floor like a dress. In the upper right corner it says, "Certain things hang on forever. Set the kids free from abuse and violence." Beside it is the Casa de Menor logo. This PSA uses strong imagery to appeal to pathos and move viewers to action by making them uncomfortable. However, even though it is effective at presenting the issue of sexual child abuse by causing the viewer to be uncomfortable, it might actually lead the viewer to disengage. This discomfort comes from the visualization of the taboo subject of sexual child abuse from within the home. Over time, sexual child abuse has been primarily conveyed as something that occurs in public areas and institutions by unfamiliar individuals.

In Casa de Menor's PSA the creators are using the audience's emotional reaction to trigger a response. The source is successful at achieving this with its depiction of sexual child abuse. The image used is unsettling to say the least, but it is because it is unsettling that it can create an emotional reaction strong enough to invoke a viewer to take action and engage in the conversation that is the prevention of sexual child abuse. A study by Hye-Jin Paek and her coauthors show that there is a direct correlation to the effectiveness of a PSA and the emotional response it creates. The emotional response as defined by Paek et al. is the first reaction the viewer has immediately after exposure. The response viewers have is usually a negative one. The emotions include ones such as anger, sadness, fear, and tension (535). From a study done by Steven J. Collings, it would show that these feelings come from the moral responsibility and pressures people feel. The most common reactions were pointing blame on the offender and on society as a whole (1069). Paek and colleagues connected these feelings and effectiveness, ". . . in a previous child abuse PSA study, negative emotions functioned as positive motivators and led directly to the audiences' decision to help" (542). It is this reasoning that emotional responses can make people take action that Casa de Menor decided to use this imagery. The girl in this PSA uses her unshakable gaze to demand the viewer to look at her. By doing so she is forcing them to also look at the abuse inflicted on her and see an issue that can be overlooked because in everyday life we cannot always see abuse. The setting in the image adds an extra layer of discomfort by portraying it within the home. Everything about this image is intentional. The organization wants viewers to feel those negative emotions because it pushes people to make those positive changes that will ultimately help decrease the amount of sexual child abuse occurring in today's society. This is why this PSA is not only effective, but important.

While there is this link between emotional response and effectiveness in PSAs, I believe that this particular PSA can also be seen as ineffective because of the emotional response it invokes. In the article by Paek et al, it talks about how negative emotions from a PSA will most likely move viewers to enact change. However, I believe the negative emotion associated with this PSA is one that will turn viewers away. Casa de Menor's projected audience is adults that are in environments where situations of sexual child abuse can occur. This would be targeting a slightly older generation from 25 and older; adults who are now in career fields where they deal with children on a day-to-day basis; or those who have families where there are children present. The issue with the current audience is that in these adults' lives sexual child abuse in the home is a subject that was avoided or was otherwise not addressed. These adults that grew up after summer 1991 are conditioned to see child abuse as an out of home event. In the study conducted on media coverage of child sexual reports by Jenny Kitzinger and Paula Skidmore, it is revealed that summer 1991 was filled with media coverage of sexual abuse, murder, and abductions of children, the attacks resulted in a mass concern about child safety from outsiders. However, not nearly as much attention was given to incidents of this nature happening in the home (51). Kitzinger and Skidmore deduced this lack of coverage as a reoccurring issue in the media. The media avoids discussing sexual child abuse in the home because it is unpleasant and often not a message people want to hear. It is easier to concentrate on strangers because people do not want to be associated with child abuse as incest (53). Promoting prevention in the home environment is difficult because of the issue of incest and the roles family is supposed to play in a child's life (54). Jean Twomey calls out the behavior of adults and how we show our younger generations that we will not deal with the issue. In Twomey's article he states, "Through our actions, inactions, what we say, and what we don't say, implicitly or explicitly encourage silence in an attempt to keep something that we do not want to exist from permeating our consciousness" (8). This is how a taboo topic is created. These are the reasons why I believe my PSA makes people uncomfortable, not only with the issue but with themselves. The viewer is forced to consider that sexual child abuse is happening, that it is happening in the home, maybe even in their own homes. While I believe Casa de Menor is shedding a much-needed light on this topic, I also feel that the audience is not prepared to look. That is why the image has such strong representation in it, so viewers can no longer ignore this issue. This why the initial emotional response viewers feel is important. Paek et al. found that emotional appeal combined with information presented in a logical, straightforward manner will allow people to have a greater recall and advance the overall effectiveness, especially among audiences with low involvement and interest (535). The audience with low involvement and interest in this case are those 25 years and older adults that need to accept that even though it was not addressed in their youth, they can impact the next generation and make changes toward these important and relevant social issues. It will take time and consistent efforts to ensure we can move towards change. The idea of consistent campaigns about awareness and prevention strategies is a common theme across research done on this topic.

In reference to my previous statements, I will acknowledge that while sexual child abuse in the home was not a prevalent topic in the media, it was not absent either. In any case, it is the context that the issue is presented in that matters. Attention to the issue of sexual child abuse primarily occurs in relation to a case. This means protection and prevention messages were not promoted until an incident occurred. Prevention strategies are often reactive rather than proactive according to Kitzinger and Skidmore (53), only being discussed when it is deemed relevant, and even then it is only discussed within the bounds of a certain case. This can be attributed to how prevention methods are not shared or talked about on a daily basis in the news (52). There was a study conducted by Dustin D. Flannery et al. that discusses how highly publicized cases on sexual abuse of adolescents effects how many incidents of sexual abuse are reported to the pediatric emergency department. Opposite to what Flannery and his co-authors expected to find, which is case reports increasing, reports actually stayed just as consistent as when there was not a case. I believe this can support my thesis that this taboo topic in the media and stereotypes associated with it is why people avoid it. It is easy to point fingers at outside invaders that prey upon these children but difficult when we realize it may be someone we know. Shame is associated with this topic when it occurs in the home. Preventative measures are not always occurring and so general awareness is not improving. In his article, Twomey points out that many victims of abuse in the home are silenced or otherwise ignored because we do not want to think about how children are being stripped of their childhood and innocence. It is also a difficult thing to talk about with a child because they can be unaware what has actually happened and must be careful to not make them too aware of this violation. The difficulties associated with addressing this issue in the home and acknowledging it has its own implications. Offenders are in a child's intimate environments where they should feel safe, and where these offenders were trusted by the central network of family and close friends. When children do speak out about their abuse, they are likely to be silenced because the trusted adult would have to confront the issue with someone they are close to and expose the individual who has committed the crime (8). This can be shown in the PSA because the girl is alone in the room. She is looking out to the audience because there is no one else to help her deal with this trauma. Her gaze can be that of a child who knows that something has happened but does not fully understand the situation and is now looking for help. It is PSAs like this that push people to think about these situations and what they should be doing about it that allows more victims to be helped. I would also like to point out that the study done on the pediatric emergency department reports was only compiled over a year. It is shown that frequency of reports increase from year to year. It is found by Paek et al that in 2002 there were 2.6 million cases reported, and then by 2005 it had increased to 3.3 million (534). This leads us back to the point of it not only being about consistency of media exposure, but also context. While there are more reports being made so more victims can receive help, if media covered prevention more frequently and within its own conversation, perhaps that would help the decline in victims as a whole.

These scholarly sources and the Casa de Menor PSA are in conversation with each other on the larger issue of the awareness of sexual child abuse in the home and how we prevent it. I have a source as old as 1995 as well as one as recent as 2017 and sources in between. My oldest and most recent sources also make similar points. What is that saying about this continuing issue? While all my sources have something to contribute, they themselves do not directly talk about this larger conversation of abuse. This is due to the discomfort about talking about sexual child abuse in the home. The fact that this overshadowing topic is tiptoed around for so many years does not better the situation. This is why we may not be ready to speak openly on this topic. However, with organizations like Casa de Menor putting out PSAs like this one we will be able to take the steps to not accept the issue but be comfortable enough to address it and more effectively prevent it from happening. This includes things like breaking down the stereotypes of the offender always being a foreign entity. If sexual child abuse in the home is the majority of cases then I ask why we are not giving it more attention. Why are we not raising more awareness? When this topic is only addressed on a case by case basis it diminishes the idea that it's happening even if it is not on the news. I agree with Kitzinger and Skidmore's conclusion that we, as a society, need to continue to raise the awareness and speak openly on how to prevent sexual child abuse in the home from occurring even when there is not a publicly addressed case on the topic. To continue to address the most common form of sexual abuse in children. To combine short-term prevention strategies and long-term prevention initiatives, we may be able to work towards a society where child sexual abuse no longer exists, not only in the outside world but in the home (47).

Works Cited

Collings, Steven J. "The Impact of Contextual Ambiguity on the Interpretation and Recall of Child Sexual Abuse Media Reports." *Journal of Interpersonal Violence,* vol. 17, no. 10, Oct. 2002, p. 1063.

Flannery, Dustin D., et al. "The Impact of High-Profile Sexual Abuse Cases in the Media on a Pediatric Emergency Department." *Journal of Child Sexual Abuse,* vol. 25, no. 6, Aug. 2016, pp. 627–635

Kitzinger, Jenny, and Paula Skidmore. "Playing Safe: Media Coverage of Child Sexual Abuse Prevention Strategies." *Child Abuse Review*, vol. 4, no. 1, Mar. 1995, pp. 47–56.

Paek, Hye-Jin, et al. "Mechanisms of Child Abuse Public Service Announcement Effectiveness: Roles of Emotional Response and Perceived Effectiveness." *Health Communication*, vol. 26, no. 6, Sept. 2011, pp. 534–545.

Twomey, Jean. "Don't Tell, Don't Ask, Don't Listen: The Trinity of Ignoring Childhood Sexual Abuse." *Brown University Child & Adolescent Behavior Letter*, vol. 33, no. 2, Feb. 2017, p. 8.

Untitled Rhetorical Analysis

Jenessa Vick, Writing 100

Can you remember the last time you lied? Most likely, it was recent. Can you remember a time you caught someone in a lie and suddenly became enraged? Or can you remember a time you were caught in a lie and felt ashamed? We all lie, and in turn, we are all lied to. Stephanie Ericsson is the author of the article, "The Ways We Lie." Within this article, Ericsson defines the various types of lies that we are all guilty of, whether their effects are serious or minimal. Ericsson wanted to bring attention to the topic of lying and how natural it is; that we do not even know we are doing it. Ericsson walks her readers through many types of lies, including definitions and examples for a better understanding. Through her article, Ericsson raises some interesting questions about the ways we lie and our morals. However, some of the claims she makes within her writing seem to weaken her argument rather than help to prove her point. Ericsson's outlook on lying seems to make sense, but some points are very shocking.

Overall, Ericsson's argument is strong, although it can be strengthened. For example, some of the claims that Ericsson makes about lies are not simply black and white. Various lies mesh together to create a whole new type of lie, which confuses readers. When Ericsson tries to back up her claim about 'ignoring the plain facts', she seems to mix two of her other examples, omission and delusion, to create this new and confusing way of lying. Omission involves, "telling most of the truth minus one or two key facts whose absence changes the story completely," while delusion is described as more of a "survival mechanism." Ericsson says that delusion is the "tendency to see excuses as facts" and "filters out information that contradicts what we want to believe." Combining these two types of lies is unnecessary because it only complicates her argument. Not only is the lie, "ignoring the plain facts," itself flawed, but so is the argument she uses to explain it. Ericsson tells the story of a priest in the 1960's who lied to himself as well as those in the community about how he sexually molested children. Both the claim and evidence used does not help her claim in the paper. At the end of the paragraph Ericsson says, "ignoring the plain facts may not in and of itself be a form of lying, but consider the context of this situation." Ericsson is making her readers do the hard work by making them decide if they believe it is a lie or not. The moment she does this, her claims weaken because readers start to doubt her.

Some of the lies that Ericsson discusses seem to be questionable about whether they are lies or not. However, she also seems to over complicate examples, which takes away her credibility. Ericsson defines "white lies" as "simple, harmless untruths," however, the example that she gives is neither simple nor harmless. Ericsson begins to tell the story of how a sergeant in Vietnam knew one of his men was killed in action but, "listed him as missing so that the man's family would receive indefinite compensation." Even though this lie was told with good intent, it is much more than a simple white lie. Everyone is familiar with the infamous 'white lie' because we are all victims of it. We pretend we didn't get that text message simply because we didn't feel like talking. Or we blame traffic for the reason why we are late to work even though we were actually in bed. White lies are small and harmless untruths we tell to spare other's feelings, and sometimes even consequences that we may face. White lies cannot extend to telling a family that their son may be alive when in reality he has died in war. Ericsson seems to be trying too hard when providing examples in her paper which go above and beyond. This supports the idea that even though Ericsson's claims are good, many of them are over thought and complex for readers to understand. These claims seem strong yet are weighed down by some faults.

Another one of Ericsson's faults is not looking at the argument through the perspective of another person. When arguing in a piece of writing, it is a fact that there will be many people who disagree with your ideas. Even though Ericsson is trying to prove her point in this article, it is necessary that she also discusses the flip side of the argument. Ericsson should include a counter argument in her article, as this would strengthen her writing greatly. If Ericsson did this, it would show readers that even though she does have firm beliefs about lying, she also knows that there is more than just one opinion. Readers would understand that Ericsson is handling the topic very maturely and can write against her argument while still effectively getting her point across. Within her article, there are many opportunities to add a contrasting opinion. When Ericsson discusses the topic of 'stereotypes and cliches' she states that it "explains a situation with just enough truth to seem unquestionable." Yet in reality, stereotypes and cliches are not lies at all, but entirely different. Stereotypes are simply ideas about groups of people that may be true or false. They include their image, how they act, what genre of music they may listen to, etc. These stereotypes tend to stick with a person due society's strong hold over our beliefs. Even though stereotypes are not always true, that does not make them lies, it just makes them inaccurate. Within stereotypes and cliches there is no action of lying, but rather a misunderstanding because of society. Ericsson's argument would have many less faults if she took the time to look at her ideas through someone else's perspective. Seeing the argument against her ideas may also sway readers to agree with her since they may not agree with the opposing ideas. If Ericsson did this, her article would appear much more concise and persuading.

Overall, Ericsson has a strong argument when it comes to her article about lying. However, there are some faults within her writing that weaken her paper. Ericsson seems very persuading, but falls short when she discusses, 'ignoring the plain facts,' 'white lies,' and 'stereotypes and cliches.' In all, Ericsson shines light on lying and that we do it very often. Lying is an action that we seem to underestimate. It is everywhere and it is much more harmful than we may realize.

Believe, Feel, Think: A Persuasive Approach to the New Jim Crow

Broderick Rheault, Writing 110

The United States of America has had one of the worst oppressive histories for people of color in the world. Starting in the colonial era, African men and women were stripped from their homes to power the American cash crop industry. They were enslaved and seen as nothing more than property. As time progressed, they were granted more rights on paper, but certain groups and state policies did everything in their power to suppress these individual freedoms. This would later be known as Jim Crow. To the average person today, it's believed that such a racial caste system couldn't possibly exist, as we live in a colorblind society. Any racial segregation was eliminated in the 1960s during the civil rights movement. However, renowned lawyer, writer, and civil rights activist, Michelle Alexander has a different perspective (About the Author). In "The New Jim Crow: Mass Incarceration in the Age of Colorblindness," she argues that Jim Crow not only still exists but has manifested itself into our incarceration system. Alexander's intent is to persuade her audience through her argument's organization. First, she presents those who don't recognize this new racial caste system with her own job experience and statistical evidence to get them to believe she is a credible source. Then she uses careful word choice to create a tone that feels inclusive of everyone involved. Finally, she gets the audience to think about the extremes of colorblindness by extending the invitation to criticism.

The premise of Alexander's article is about how the current incarceration system has taken on the roles of the seemingly outdated Jim Crow. She starts her article following the timeline for voting rights of an African American family; with Jarvious Cotton being the most recent member of eligible voting age. Slavery, Homicide, Klan intimidation, literacy tests, and poll taxes have all prohibited his ancestors from exercising their basic rights. Jarvious was denied the right to vote because he is considered a felon (Alexander 261). Alexander explains that felons are subject to all the forms of discrimination that thrived during the era of Jim Crow: employment discrimination, housing discrimination, denial of the right to vote, denial of educational opportunity, denial of food stamps and other public benefits, and exclusion from jury service (262–63). She goes on further, explaining that the majority of felons are African Americans by no coincidence. During the War on Drugs, incarceration rates increased at record levels with the majority being black Americans (Alexander 267–68). Mass stereotyping, created by the media, led to the idea that most black men are criminals; and because criminals are legally segregated then the majority of black men are coincidentally still under the same oppression as were the blacks in the era of Jim Crow (Alexander 267).

Failure to recognize this racial segregation due to the notion that people are people, not colors, is the reason why Alexander wrote this book. Her purpose is to persuade those who are colorblind, specifically those who oppose her view, that denying incarceration stereotypes and avoiding racial discussion is only worsening the problem. To accomplish this, Alexander must be very careful with the way she portrays herself in her argument. She must build it in a distinct way that causes her critics to believe in her as a credible source, feel how she does on the issue, and allow them to think about the problem themselves. Failure to do so in this order could render her arguments effectiveness obsolete. Ultimately, she wants her audience to see that it's all of our responsibilities to take the time to deal with this issue head on before this period of time is referenced in a history book as another civil rights crisis (Alexander 272).

The foundation Alexander uses to get her audience to believe in her is by establishing herself as a source of credibility. Towards the beginning of the book, she describes the moment when she first encountered the idea of a racial caste system in the United States. As she was stepping onto the bus, a poster with the words, "The Drug War Is The New Jim Crow," caught her eye (Alexander 264). What's important to note is where she was heading. According to the text she, "Was heading to her new job, director of the Racial Justice Project of the American Civil Liberties Union (ACLU) in Northern California" (Alexander 265). For those that don't know, this is a large organization with over 2 million members, whose goal is to defend the constitutional rights of all individuals (ACLU). Informing her audience that she was a director at such a large organization for civil rights shows that she must be well versed in civil law. In addition, Alexander tells the reader in the following paragraph that she is a lawyer who has litigated many "class-action employment discrimination cases" (265). Effectively showing the audience a resume of her experience. This is a potent foundation because the idea that the incarceration system is a racial caste system falls under the category of civil law. The experience she has had in this content area shows someone who doubts her claims of colorblindness being the problem, that she isn't making broad claims about a topic she knows little about. Instead it will make these people believe that she is a credible source, who is making claims based on her prior knowledge in this field. Now this alone will certainly not change their minds, but it encourages them to accept Alexanders facts because they are listening to an expert on the subject.

Building off of her credibility, Alexander uses statistical evidence to demonstrate the rise in incarceration rates in the United States. About midway through her book she is discussing how the War on Drugs has helped Jim Crow manifest itself into our incarceration system. She immediately compliments this with the following information; "In less than thirty years, the US penal population exploded from around 300,000 to more than 2 million. With drug convictions accounting for the majority of the increase" (Alexander 268). Then, in the next sentence she writes that the United States has the highest incarceration rate in the world with roughly 750 prisoners per 100,000 people (Alexander 269). She even goes on to say that this is larger than a repressive regime like China (Alexander 269). The author chooses to compare the U.S. incarceration rates to China to show how drastically this rate has risen. Those who oppose the idea that the United States' rise in incarcerations has anything to do with a racial caste may suggest the rise was caused by an increase in population. According to BBC, China's prison population per 100,000 people is about 130 (In Depth). This number doesn't sound significant until you compare it to their total population: around 1.38 billion people (U.S. Census Bureau Current Population). The United States only has a population of around 330 million (U.S. Census Bureau Current Population). To put this into perspective China has a population that is roughly 1.05 billion more the U.S., but the United States has about 620 more inmates per 100,000 people. Alexander is showing her critics that the United States has a significantly higher ratio of incarcerations than the rest of the world, and it is by no coincidence. Now it is important to note that having numbers doesn't guarantee that Alexander's opposition will completely agree since numbers can be disputed and interpreted differently. However, by providing statistical evidence it gives her argument a secondary source of credibility. Now her argument is also based on actual trends and numbers rather than just "taking her word for it." For the people who don't believe that the United States has a large incarceration rate, she has presented them with physical evidence that may change their mind.

Now that Alexander has gotten her audience to believe her as a credible source, she then uses selective word choice to create an inclusive tone in her writing. Towards the end of the book she is discussing the fear associated with talking about a possible caste still existing in the United States. In her statement, Alexander writes, "We avoid talking about caste in our society because we are ashamed of our history" (Alexander 270). Alexander makes the point to use pronouns like "we" and "our." Effectively what she's doing is informing her audience that as an American woman of color, this is just as much her responsibility as it would be someone else's. In her case, Alexander must use these specific pronouns to steer around potential bias surrounding her ethnic background. Due to the color of her skin, and that she is arguing about a new racial caste that is targeting mostly African Americans, those who oppose the system's existence may suggest that she is calling on others to solve an issue that seems isolated within the black community. This may cause her critics to stop listening to her argument if they feel like the burden has been placed on them. In response to this Alexander creates inclusivity to help eliminate the potential for someone to interpret her work as condescending. By eliminating this superiority complex, it may increase the chances that her audience listens to what she is trying to say. No one is going to want to listen to her argument if it sounds like she is demanding others to fix the problem, effectively contradicting the whole idea of equality. Instead she wants those who are colorblind to see that she, as well as other people of color, have contributed to this problem, and now it's time that collectively a solution must be brought forward.

After the author presented her evidence, she invites the audience to think about the extremes of colorblindness. At the start of her closing paragraphs she writes, "Skepticism about the claims made here is warranted . . . Failure to acknowledge the relevant differences, as well as their implications, would be a disservice to racial justice discourse" (Alexander 271). The invitation to skepticism was an intentional move. Alexander is making a very pronounced claim when discussing the possibility of the U.S. government implementing a racial caste into our incarceration system during the War on Drugs(267–68). She wants her audience to realize that it's natural to be unconvinced by such a powerful allegation, especially because it's the same response she had. The entire reason she explains her encounter with the Jim Crow poster early on, is to set the stage for her initial stance on the issue (Alexander 264–65). She personally thought the idea was abstract, until she later convinced herself through thorough research. Alexander's use of her own story is meant to open up an internal discussion for her opposition. She isn't expecting them to change their mind right away, but rather think about the issue for themselves. It's unreasonable for anyone to read one source of information and immediately change their views to mirror what they have just read. If those who refuse to see colorblindness as concealing this new racial caste system, do not contemplate Alexander's argument, but rather just blindly agree with it, then no progress has been made. To reinforce her point, she needs the people that disagree with her to explore the topic and convince themselves for any progress to be made. Alexander is also trying to suggest that believing her claim to the extreme would contradict the whole argument itself. She wants the audience to think about the information she has presented from a realistic perspective. Not all black men have been wrongfully convicted of felonies, but there are those who have been. She extends the invitation to criticism to get her audience to take a second to think about her claims from both perspectives. This will help persuade them in the long run because their bias is no longer blocking out her point of view.

In her book, Alexander is on a mission to persuade those who are colorblind that Jim Crow has manifested itself into our incarceration system. She wants these individuals to understand how viewing our current system like this is only making this racial caste worse. To persuade this audience she systematically crafts her argument to build off itself using the structure believe, feel, think. She starts off by presenting herself as a credible source. By establishing this sense of credibility, the audience has no choice but to see that she is not just some average person who knows very little about her argument. Rather her profession has enveloped her with a lot of experience on the topic. After she establishes that she is a credible source, she presents statistical evidence to show her audience proof for her claims. Now that her audience can believe her, she uses careful word selection. This is to avoid sounding condescending, which could lead the reader to stop listening to her perspective. By including herself as part of the problem, she eliminates that sense of superiority her critics may perceive because she is a woman of color. Finally, she encourages the audience to think for themselves. This part is more open ended, but by having healthy skepticism of her claims and an understanding of its extremes, it causes her audience to look into the issue themselves which can make them more receptive to her point of view. If the author were to change this believe, feel, think structure, it would lose its persuasive effectiveness. By not establishing the foundation that she is a credible source, her opposition would not be as easily persuaded by her word choice. Eliminating the sense of superiority wouldn't persuade them if they felt like she didn't have a credible claim in the first place. This same logic would apply to the last step. If she invited criticism into her claims without presenting credibility and an inclusive tone on her part, then the audience would just continue to see the incarceration system from the same colorblind lens. Alexander has developed an effective, well-crafted strategy for presenting her argument. By using the specific order of believe, feel, think she presents a stronger case that will help persuade her audience.

Work Cited

"About the ACLU." *American Civil Liberties Union*, American Civil Liberties Union, www.aclu.org/about-aclu.

"About the Author." *The New Jim Crow*, newjimcrow.com/about-the-author.

Alexander, Michelle, and Cathy Birkenstein. "The New Jim Crow: Mass Incarceration in the Age of Colorblindness." *They Say, I Say*, edited by Gerald Graff, 4th ed., W. W. Norton & Company, 2018, pp. 261–274.

"In Depth." *BBC News*, BBC, 20 June 2005, news.bbc.co.uk/2/shared/spl/hi/uk/06/prisons/html/nn2page1.stm.

"U.S. Census Bureau Current Population." *Census Bureau QuickFacts*, 8 Oct. 2018, www.census.gov/popclock/print.php?component=counter.

Research Reports and Annotated Bibliography

Annotated Bibliography

Janay Wynter, Writing 110

Hairston, Tiffany R., et al. "Counselor Education Students' Perceptions of Wellness and Mental Health in African American Men: The Effects of Colorism." *Journal of Multicultural Counseling and Development*, vol. 46, no. 3, 2018, pp. 171–185.

Summary: In this article, Hairston explain why colorism has such a huge impact on the African American community and conducts an experiment to test his theories. He states that colorism can be more hurtful than racism to African Americans because colorism can come from non–African Americans but also from those of the same race. For her research, Hairston collected data from seven universities in Ohio and recruited 155 students from different universities to complete surveys. She concludes the article by stating her implications and explaining what she could change for future research to get better results.

Evaluation: Tiffany Harriston works at the school of intervention and wellness at the University of Toledo and Unison Health in Ohio. I believe this source is credible because she is qualified to conduct the research explained in the article. She also thoroughly explained every variable that she took into account when conducting her studies.

Plan for Use: I plan to use Hariston's research to explain why the jokes made in Martin could have had such a negative impact on some of the show's viewers. I will use portions of Hariston's data, along with some quotes or references from her introductory paragraphs where she explains why colorism from within the black community can have a bigger impact than when it comes from non-African Americans

Scott, Mack. "From Blackface to Beulah: Subtle Subversion in Early Black Sitcoms." *Journal of Contemporary History*, vol. 49, no. 4, 2014, pp. 743–769.

Summary: In this article, Scott discusses early black sitcoms on television such as, *The Cosby Show*. While acknowledging the fact that these sitcoms often instilled colorist, racist, and often sexist views, he points out that they played a major role in humanizing the African American community to white American. He notes that most of these African American actors were only able to make black family sitcoms so widely acceptable and respected among the majority of TV viewers by conforming to these colorist ideas. He explains the positive impacts that these shows had on black people in the media.

Evaluation: I'm still not completely sure if this article is a scholarly article, but Scott has many credible sources and contributors so I do think that the piece itself is credible. He analyzes each of the shows and comments on how they each played a part in changing how black people were portrayed in the media.

Plan for Use: I plan to use this article to help establish the importance of Martin and the messages expressed in the show. I will use Scott's research to explain how black sitcoms had an impact on how African Americans were viewed by others in society, and therefore the messages and ideas that were expressed within the shows were equally as important and influential.

Thompson, Maxine S, and Verna M Keith. "THE BLACKER THE BERRY: Gender, Skin Tone, Self-Esteem, and Self-Efficacy." *Gender & Society*, vol. 15, no. 3, 2001, pp. 336–357.

Summary: In this article, Thompson and Keith explain the negative effects that colorism and racism have on black men and women's self-esteem and self-efficacy. They comment on how these factors affect men and women differently. They then share their studies and explain every variable that they took into account while conducting their research. They conclude the article by summing up their results using their findings to explain why perception of skin color has such a negative impact on people of color.

Evaluation: In addition to this being a peer-reviewed article, both authors of this work for credible universities. These credentials, along with their data and methods used in their research, lead me to trust this source for my paper.

Plan for Use: After doing thorough research on the black people they were testing, Keith and Thompson came to the conclusion that skin tone has negative effects on both self-esteem and self-efficacy but affects men and women differently. They also found that those who had lower self-esteem scores were dark-skinned women. I plan to use Thompson and Keith's research and results to further support my claim that the comedic digs at darker skinned black women on Martin more than likely had a negative impact on the show's audience.

Townsend, Tiffany G, et al. "I'm No Jezebel; I Am Young, Gifted, and Black: Identity, Sexuality, and Black Girls." *Psychology of Women Quarterly*, vol. 34, no. 3, 2010, pp. 273–285.

Summary: In this article, Townsend explains the effects that colorism and explains how the concept ties into the history of the sexualization of African American women. She explains how these have an impact on young, black women's sexual identities and personal image. She then explains her research in which she studied a sample of 270 African American girls to test if colorism and certain stereotypes has an impact on their sexual activity (safe sex) and sense of self. The article concludes with Townsend sharing the results of her research.

Evaluation: Tiffany G. Townsend works in the Department of Psychiatry at Georgetown University Medical School. She thoroughly explains all of her research and methods, as well as her findings which she then applies to real life. This article is definitely scholarly and credible. The information that Townsend provides is also useful to my research.

Plan for Use: This article uses research that I can utilize to strengthen my argument and paper. Townsend's article applies actual research to the concept of colorism and the impact that it can have on young women of color. I plan to use her research to support my argument that *Martin* had a negative impact on the black community, but black women specifically.

Undergraduate Procrastination

Breanna Formanski, Writing 110

Abstract: A majority of undergraduate students all around the world have procrastinated at least once in their career as a student. The problem with procrastination though is that it is not just holding off on one or two assignments, a large number of these undergraduates tend to do it on many of their assignments, if not all of them. Waiting to do assignments isn't only a bad idea for someone's sleep schedule, because their staying up late the night before to complete their work, but it also can have a very negative effect on students' grades. The outcome will be poor, even if the student believes their best work only happens at the last minute, because many people truly believe that. Throughout this report, many questions involving procrastination will be answered, and the most important answer includes tips on how to resolve undergraduates issue of procrastinating.

Report:

I. Purpose

In today's society, it's vital to have an adequate understanding of how to ward off procrastination tendencies. The hard-hitting question is: How do undergraduates push themselves to prevent procrastination on assignments? This question is important because undergraduates all across America allow their stress to build up which ultimately leads to their struggle with procrastinating. Although it may not seem like a big issue and the habit can easily be blamed on laziness, procrastination has become so much more; it has become something that students justify as being acceptable because they know that the assignment will get done even if it is at the last possible minute. The problem with waiting, though, is that grades will suffer because of it.

II. Methods

The article that proved itself to be the most useful throughout the research is entitled, "Learning How to Learn: A Student Success Course for At Risk Students." The credit for this well structured article goes to three authors, Elizabeth R. Bowering, Joanne Mills, and Allison Merrit, making the lead author, Bowering. This article was the most useful for this report because the authors introduced a way to prevent procrastination that no other article had. Their tactic is just simply the idea of forming a positive professor to student relationship. They describe this as being beneficial because that relationship had proven to help students better "organize their time, avoid procrastination, and manage test anxiety."

III. Findings

Procrastination is defined in a few different ways. First, Eric S. Cerino from Eastern Connecticut State University defined it as "freely postponing an action with the awareness of the detriment it may cause in the future" (156). Second, Rannveig Grom Saele, et al. described procrastination as an "involuntary but irrational delay of an intended course of action, with non-beneficial consequences" (758). From these viewpoints, there is a common theme of pushing off assignments until the last possible minute. Among the common factors that help undergraduates prevent procrastination, three are the most helpful:

having a strategic learning approach, a positive professor/student relationship, and self efficacy.

But, what causes procrastination in the first place? M. Betul Yilmaz shared that roughly 80 percent of students admitted to being involved with procrastination at some point or another. What may come as a shock, though, is that more than 50 percent of them are consistent and commonly known procrastinators. Undergraduates justify procrastination as being okay because they know that their assignment will get done at some point, even if that means that they're pulling an all-nighter the night before it is due. It will get done at any cost, but they will also push it off as long as they possibly can. Along with this theory, Yilmaz also stated that students would rather hold off on their assignment until right before it's due, rather than following a scheduled process. Some undergrads may even say that they do their best work at the last minute while they feel rushed. Many even believe that if an assignment is difficult, then there's more reason for them to put it off (Datig and Herkner).

Having a strategic learning approach can help with putting off assignments. This is due to the simple fact that if the student is learning correctly, then there's no reason assignments should be put off if it isn't as difficult (Datig and Herkner). The more difficult it is poses as a reason to put it off further because Datig and Herkner shared that "more that 85% of all students across the disciplines experience writing difficulties at some point during their university career" (128). The strategic learning approach is seen as a positive form of self-regulation (Saele). Saele mentions a few different types of learning approaches as well. He states that the first one, the surface learning approach, occurs when students focus on only reproduction and memorization. Rather than fully understanding the meanings and having a deeper grasp of certain concepts, some students will only focus on memorizing the needed material just to be able to pass exams due to their fear of failure.

A second, more intensive, approach is described as the deep learning approach. This type of approach would mean that the student has a deeper desire to fully understand the content that they're reading. It is shared with the readers, by Saele, that this approach is "characterized by an interest and a search for meaning and comprehension" (758). This student would not completely follow the syllabus because they are more specifically focused on their comprehension of the subject, rather than focusing on the idea of passing upcoming exams.

The third and final approach is referred to as the strategic learning approach. The student who practices strategic learning has a tendency to combine the two previously mentioned approaches to make a perfected tactic. This undergraduate would find themselves having both a deep understanding of their material and is equally prepared for exams. The deciding factor upon which approach to use would be dependent on the task at hand. Students who use the strategic learning approach are told to be "good at time management, study organization and progress monitoring" (758). These undergrads are also the ones who embrace the skills of study organization and progress monitoring. Some of these students even have a good relationship with their professors.

Having a good relationship with the professor can be a key way to crush a bad procrastination habit. A good professor to student relationship helps with procrastination because students are more likely to be supplied with helpful tips directly from their professor. In other words, the undergraduate student can be provided with "guidance and constructive feedback" (Bowering). These tips could then help the student be placed on the right track for their assignments to come. Being placed on the right track instantly empowers one to get their work done the right way; the right way being that they're doing it adequately and to a defined schedule. The confidence instilled by their professor will allow relationship building to occur which then influences the likelihood of attaining academic success (Bowering).

Being able to form a good relationship with some professors can make students more willing to get their work done in a sufficient amount of time. Many may feel that their relationship makes them more willing to complete their tasks. These undergraduates may not necessarily like the class, but because they like their teacher, the bond essentially makes them want to do their assignment adequately for their teacher. The students' motivation could be because they don't want to ruin that bond or simply because that professor might actually make the given information interesting. According to Bowering, a good professor/student relationship is told to give an "enhanced understanding of learning strategies, sharpened time management techniques, and decreased test anxiety" (10). This relationship can also provide students with a possible greater enjoyment throughout the semester and an even better final grade.

To support the relationship with a professor further, students surprisingly enjoyed having good relationships with their professors. This valued relationship can ultimately help with many things throughout the course of the semester. Some benefits can include things like not being scared to use professor office hours, or to sit at the front of the classroom, and to make proactive comments throughout the course. Many undergraduates find their instructors to be intimidating, but by doing both of these things, the given information is better received and that normally goes hand-in-hand with having a good grade in the class. Even being able to make proactive comments towards the teacher about the course can not only benefit that student but it can provide for the entire class as well. Bowering even said that, "students consistently commented on the course evaluations that their relationship with the instructor was a valued part of their experience" (10).

The third key way for undergraduates to prevent themselves from procrastination habits is through self-efficacy. Self-efficacy is defined as "the belief in a person's ability in specific scenarios such as believing in their capability to perform a task or learn given information" (Cerino). This term also shows an individual's confidence through their ability to apply control over their own motivation, behavior and even their social environment. Cerino states that this specific style is a resolution to procrastination because it "refers to a lot of time and consideration put into schoolwork, studying, and time management for optimal results" (157). Those who have high levels of self-efficacy also reported that they had higher goals that they were aiming to achieve through their own academic motivation.

Self-efficacy can easily influence one's levels of procrastination. This is explained by the fact that it is described as a source of self motivation which any individual can have because it can be a self-discipline that a student, or anyone for that matter can train themselves to do (Cerino). According to Cerino, self-efficacy and procrastination are surprisingly closely related due to the fact that they can both influence one's schoolwork immensely; it just depends whether the student allows there to be a negative effect or a positive one. The two are also strongly tied into each other because research has shown that several forms of motivation and self-efficacy have been predictors of procrastination. This close relationship showed that "students who lacked academic motivation entirely tended to procrastinate more on academic tasks" (161).

Ultimately, to prevent procrastination, there must be a strong relationship when it comes to all three key points. Undergraduates must have a strategic learning approach to be sure that oneself has a proper form of learning. They must have a good relationship with their instructor; this will ensure that they are allowing themselves to absorb all of the knowledge they can possibly receive through the use of professors office hours, sitting at the front of the class and by having proactive comments and feedback for the instructors course. Lastly, it is essential to train oneself to have self-efficacy. This last point of total confidence will ensure the outcome of a good final grade. If a student can live by all three, then that undergraduate should never find themselves in a hard place due to their habit of procrastination.

IV. Discussion

Procrastination has become a much bigger issue than many might have originally thought. This report has proved though that there are ways around it, and ways to defeat procrastination head-on. As stated in the conclusion, if a student can live by all three of the procrastination prevention tactics provided in this report, then for that individual, procrastination may never be a problem for them again. To reflect upon this idea though, I personally struggle with procrastination habits and one might question how to begin the process of defeating their procrastination. There may never be an ideal time to start, because then waiting for that time may also provide an excuse to continue with procrastination habits until the time arrives. Undergraduates must fully engulf themselves in all three prevention theories, but the thing to always remember is that all three don't come at the same time. It can be a slow approach of trying out each practice one by one, and eventually allowing all three forces to join together.

Some may be skeptical about the powers of procrastination and the way that it can take a toll on students, especially for parents or guardians. Parents and guardians usually do not understand why their child is procrastinating the way they do, depending on their severity, but as previously shared throughout the report, the build-up of stress is a noticeable cause of procrastination, which is something that is very common but very hard to deal with at the same time. These skeptical parents, may not understand how stress can lead to procrastination either because another concept that was previously mentioned is that many just believe students are lazy. Procrastination is a real problem that has many other causes aside from stress, but every individual can grow from their habits as long as they try the three steps to procrastination prevention which is having a strategic learning approach, a positive professor/student relationship, and self efficacy.

Works Cited

Bowering, Elizabeth R., et al. "Learning How to Learn: A Student Success Course for At Risk Students." *Canadian Journal for the Scholarship of Teaching and Learning*, June 2017, pp. 1–16., doi:10.5206/cjsotl-rcacea.2017.3.12.

Cerino, Eric S. "Relationships Between Academic Motivation, Self-Efficacy, and Academic Procrastination." *Psi Chi Journal of Psychological Research*, vol. 19, no. 4, 2014, pp. 156–163., doi:10.24839/2164-8204.jn19.4.156.

Datig, Ilka, and Luise Herkner. "Get Ready For A Long Night: Collaborating With The Writing Center To Combat Student Procrastination." *Crln.Acrl.Org*, 2014, http://crln.acrl.org/index.php/crlnews/article/view/9086/9960. Accessed 27 Nov 2018.

Sæle, Rannveig Grøm, et al. "Relationships between Learning Approach, Procrastination and Academic Achievement amongst First-Year University Students." *Higher Education*, vol. 74, no. 5, 2016, pp. 757–774, doi:10.1007/s10734-016-0075-z.

Yilmaz, M. Betul. "The Relation between Academic Procrastination of University Students and Their Assignment and Exam Performances: The Situation in Distance and Face-to-Face Learning Environments." *Journal of Education and Training Studies*, vol. 5, no. 9, 2017, p. 146-157, doi:10.11114/jets.v5i9.2545.

Women in STEM: The Impact of Increasing the Number of Women in the Field

Kei Jahaj, Writing 110

Abstract

This study focuses on the research question: To what extent would greater numbers of women who pursue a career in STEM have a positive impact on the field? After investigating this question the thesis is: Increasing the number of women in the STEM workforce would improve the customer service, better the atmosphere in the workplace and promote a more democratic decision making in an organization or a family matter. An interesting finding about the topic is that if the number of women who work in the STEM field would be increased, technological companies could create $470 to $579 billion value, and could add 1.2% to 1.6% to national gross domestic product. Furthermore, studies showed that diversity assists into creating a more exciting workplace and a diverse way of thinking, which enhances learning while benefiting progressive innovations and economic growth.

I. Purpose

This research question matters to every person who is interested into following a career in STEM because diversity in the field would influence different aspects of their profession. Women represent half of the world population, yet most of them do not professionally engage in high-earning STEM degrees, which creates a big gender gap that makes females overlooked. A greater women workforce in the department would change competition, innovation and creativity. With more diversity on the field, the scientific and technological products would represent a wider range of users, by a broader span of experiences.

II. Methods

The most valuable article was: "U.S. Science and Engineering Workforce: Underrepresentation of Women and Minorities" by Roli Varma. This article shows that technological companies that embrace diversity in their workforce would gain economic growth. The author gives statistics about the amount of worth that the company would gain, which includes "$470 to $579 billion value, and could add 1.2% to 1.6% to national gross domestic product" (695). The author has a Ph.D. in Science and Technology Studies, as well as a M.S. in Science, Technology and Values. Varma is the author of two books, 53 journal articles, three edited journals, and 11 book chapters.

III. Findings

Careers in science, technology, engineering and mathematics (STEM) are constantly evolving, while including a wide range of high-paying professions one can pursue. However, the number of women who work on the STEM fields is very low, compared to men, which creates a disproportionate representation in these important areas of life. This unbalanced gender diversity results in men dominating the processes, politics and beliefs in the field. The underrepresentation of females has a broad impact, as it assists in creating stereotypes, and provides men with more power in decision making. Even though the number of women in the workforce has increased these last few years, the new jobs are preferably offered to men. Increasing the number of women in the STEM workforce would improve the customer service, better the atmosphere in the workplace and promote a more democratic decision-making in an organization or a family matter.

The number of women in STEM fields is really low. A study by Varma showed that in 2013, women made up only 15% of engineers. 8% of them were mechanical engineers and about 11% to 12% included electrical, computer, aerospace, aeronautical, and astronautical engineers. Low number of female participation is also seen in physics occupations, where women constitute only 11% of physicists and astronomers. Women made up 24% of computer and information scientists. Diversity was greater among life scientists where women made up 48% of population (693).

Equal representation of women in the field would represent a wider range of product users. Technology and science is evolving really quickly, creating new inventions which have a great impact on our lives. In most cases, women remain users of the benefits that the male-dominant, high-technology society offers. The absence of women in designing and producing the scientific and technological products, results in missing out new innovative ideas from a different point of view (Varma 695). Women come from different backgrounds and experiences, and differ from men in the way of thinking. By that means, including women into the inventing process will lead to a broader range of products for the user. Not hiring women in a company may result in missing out on talented workers, who are able to give diverse perspectives into problem solving. Companies would be able to increase effectiveness of their products, because they would be willing to understand more in depth the concerns that their customers have.

A company that increases the number of women in their workforce would be able to benefit more from its customers and the other way around. As women are able to include a more diverse group of product users, improving the gender gap in a company "could create $470 to $579 billion in value for the technology company, and could add 1.2% to 1.6% to national gross domestic product" (Varma 695). These statistics show that having more women in a technological company is beneficial for the business. As the business grows, there is place for bigger investments to create new products. These innovations would improve the life of the customer. To conclude, higher number of females in a company does not only benefit the company itself economically, but it also benefits the user in terms of improving their experience with the new products on the market.

Increasing the number of women would improve the company's products and procedures. By tapping into the talents of both genders, companies can improve the customer service. Women are as capable as men or even more to succeed in STEM, therefore a greater number of females on the field gives a new perspective which positively affects the user's satisfaction with the new products. The study by Stoet and Geary showed how "girls performed similarly or better than boys on generic science literacy tests" (591). This claim indicates that women have a more powerful ability into analyzing and understanding more complex scientific problems than men.

Not only products, but also processes, improve when companies include more females in their workforce. Groups with equal representation of both genders and groups with a greater number of women than men, "perform better than homogeneous groups on a management simulation task, and this effect [is] explained by more effective collaborative group processes and cooperative norms" (Bear and Woolley 148). As a result, if the number of females would be greater in a company, the procedures of developing a product would be more precise. As a consequence users would have more effective innovations, which better complete their needs in life.

A higher representation of women in STEM would increase the satisfaction of all workers in the workplace and obliterate gender bias. Having more female role models, encourages women to sympathize with them and assist in getting rid of gender assumptions. Improving diversity in the field is "essential for creating a thriving workplace, diverse way of thinking and enhanced learning that elevates excellence and benefits scientific innovation and economic growth"(Smith et al. 1087). By this conclusion, Smith et.al suggest that in order for progress of the field and a more dynamic workplace, the equal representation of women is required.

Moreover, greater numbers of women would benefit the female workers themselves. Women usually find it easy to relate to other women scientists of the field, in terms of gender bias, discrimination, and not being treated fairly, because "when people feel empathic concern for a person facing hardship, they conclude they must also have a bond with this person" (Pietri et al. 193). As a conclusion, women identify themselves with all women scientists, which encourages their interest in STEM. In these terms, increasing the number of women in the workforce will actually decrease gender bias, as women will have more successful role models to look up to.

A greater number of women in STEM would assist in a more unbiased decision-making process. Females have low power in decision making, which causes this process to be biased, as men dominate the field. The reason that female have low power, is because of their underrepresentation in STEM. Therefore, increasing the number of women in the workforce would also increase their capability to make decisions. The importance of power consists into facilitating "both agentic goals, because it leads to individual recognition and achievement, and communal goals, because it enables interpersonal communication and relationships" (Chen and Moons 117). Chen and Moons suggest that having power to make decisions allows forming social connections and acknowledges one's performance at a certain job. Thus, the process would be more democratic as it includes a wider range of participants, from different experiences, despite their gender.

A greater number of women in STEM would reconstruct the power females have in decision-making in family enterprises. STEM jobs are some of the highest paying ones in the business world. In the case that only men are exposed to the benefits of earning a high salary, women are left with limited or no power in the family and, therefore, they are overlooked. The way the society is constructed is that "the social positioning (i.e. social status and autonomy) of women in the household facilitates women's access to and decision-making power related to family planning" (Reed et al. 1204). In other words, the economical state gives one a greater ability to make decisions in the family and be seen as more potent. If the female workforce in the field would be increased, more women would be beneficiaries of the high-earning payments. As a consequence, women would be more independent and have a significant capability of making important decisions in the family.

Increasing the number of women in the STEM workforce overall would have a positive impact on the field. Customer service would improve as diversity on the field makes it able to incorporate a broader range of users, and also betters their experience in the use of the innovations. A higher representation of women in the field would also improve the atmosphere in the workplace and eliminate gender bias. A higher number of women in STEM would assist in a more democratic decision making, as an equitable process includes opinions and achievements of both, male and female. A greater number of women in STEM would expose them to high-earning jobs, and as a consequence they would have more power into making decisions in the family.

IV. Discussion

Using evidence from the journal articles, it is confirmed that increasing the number of women in STEM has a positive impact on the field. Across seven articles, it was found that women can improve the atmosphere on the workplace, as increasing the number of women in the workforce would decrease gender bias, and women would have more successful role models to look up to. Furthermore, the customer service would be better, as a diverse way of thinking would result into innovations that would better the experience of the user and it would incorporate a broader range of customers. The decision-making process in the workplace and in family would be more democratic, as the gap between man and women would decrease.

Further recommendations include attempts to increase the number of women in STEM. Women should be introduced to real-world problems into coursework and extracurricular activities. Opportunities for mentorship and accepting community should also be provided. Also, anyone in an academic role can influence a student's decision to stay in or choose STEM as a career, so academic leadership must be willing to help women, despite gender bias.

Works Cited

Bear, Julia B., and Anita Williams Woolley. "The Role of Gender in Team Collaboration and Performance." *Interdisciplinary Science Reviews*, vol. 36, no. 2, June 2011, pp. 146–153. Academic Search Premier, doi:10.1179/030801811X13013181961473.

Chen, Jacqueline M., and Wesley G. Moons. "They Won't Listen to Me: Anticipated Power andWomen's Disinterest in Male-Dominated Domains." *Group Processes & Intergroup Relations*, vol. 18, no. 1, Jan. 2015, pp. 116–128. Academic Search Premier, doi:10.1177/1368430214550340.

Pietri, Evava S., et al. "Maybe She Is Relatable." *Psychology of Women Quarterly*, vol. 42, no. 2, June 2018, pp. 192–219. Academic Search Premier, doi:10.1177/0361684317752643.

Reed, Elizabeth, et al. "Access to Money and Relation to Women's Use of Family Planning Methods Among Young Married Women in Rural India." *Maternal & Child Health Journal*, vol. 20, no. 6, June 2016, pp. 1203–1210. Academic Search Premier, doi:10.1007/s10995-016-1921-4.

Smith, Jessi L., et al. "Now Hiring! Empirically Testing a Three-Step Intervention to Increase Faculty Gender Diversity in STEM." *BioScience*, vol. 65, no. 11, Nov. 2015, pp. 1084–1087. Academic Search Premier, doi:10.1093/biosci/biv138.

Stoet, Gijsbert, and David C. Geary. "The Gender-Equality Paradox in Science, Technology, Engineering, and Mathematics Education." *Psychological Science* (0956-7976), vol. 29, no. 4, Apr. 2018, pp. 581–593. Academic Search Premier, doi:10.1177/0956797617741719.

Varma, Roli "U.S. Science and Engineering Workforce: Underrepresentation of Women and Minorities." *American Behavioral Scientist*, vol. 62, no. 5, May 2018, pp. 692–697. Academic Search Premier, doi:10.1177/0002764218768847.